Laugh and the World Laughs with You

Greatest Clean Joke Book Ever

. . . I Think!

By the fascinating joke-teller and puzzle-man.
MICHAEL P. MC CRORY

GREATEST CLEAN JOKE BOOK EVER . . . I THINK!

Copyright © 2019 Michael P. Mc Crory.

All rights reserved. No part of this book may be used or reproduced by any means, graphic, electronic, or mechanical, including photocopying, recording, taping or by any information storage retrieval system without the written permission of the author except in the case of brief quotations embodied in critical articles and reviews.

iUniverse books may be ordered through booksellers or by contacting:

iUniverse
1663 Liberty Drive
Bloomington, IN 47403
www.iuniverse.com
1-800-Authors (1-800-288-4677)

Because of the dynamic nature of the Internet, any web addresses or links contained in this book may have changed since publication and may no longer be valid. The views expressed in this work are solely those of the author and do not necessarily reflect the views of the publisher, and the publisher hereby disclaims any responsibility for them.

Any people depicted in stock imagery provided by Getty Images are models,
and such images are being used for illustrative purposes only.
Certain stock imagery © Getty Images.

ISBN: 978-1-5320-6742-6 (sc)
ISBN: 978-1-5320-6741-9 (e)

Library of Congress Control Number: 2019900955

Print information available on the last page.

iUniverse rev. date: 02/28/2019

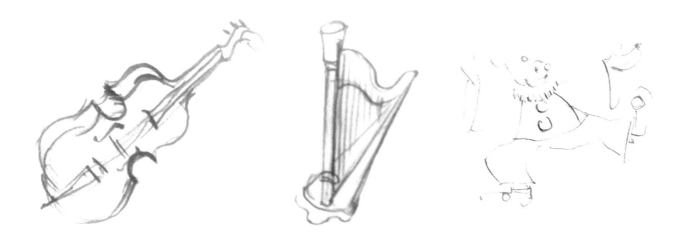

For the good are always the merry, save by an evil chance. And the merry love the fiddle, and the merry love to dance.

How often we hear the words:

"…but I can never remember jokes."

No need to now; they're all here for you.

These clean jokes will last you three lifetimes.

Composed by:
Michael P. Mc Crory
Edited by:
Michael P. Mc Crory.
Artwork by:
Mariola K. Paini MFA
Artist to the Saints.

They say that hard work never killed anyone, but why risk it?

Oh, come ye back to Ireland when life was hard but simpler

Introduction

Laughter is like an elixir from God given to us as a way to relieve stress, escape into a world of bliss, and simply make the everyday struggles of life seem less bothersome. Mark Twain once remarked, "Humor is a great leveler."

I find it so interesting that people can gather around anyone that can muster up a joke in a crowd and create a sort of camaraderie of the crowd that brings everyone together. The fact that both women and men are attracted to anyone that can keep them laughing is a testament to why we all need humor. How nice if we could all inject humor into our everyday situations.

People want to laugh and avoid the things that make them cry. The whole intent and purpose of this book is to bring joy to your life and make your day more cheerful. It is a compilation of years of studying what makes people laugh and learning what jokes put a smile on your face and joy in your heart, without the need to be vulgar or launch personal attacks that demean and de- grade our fellow man. It is also a book that demonstrates that we all need to be able to not take ourselves too seriously and to allow humor to heal our personal anxieties. At the moment of laughter all masks come off; we have moved out of the doldrums of life; moved out of the regularity of our lives; moved to an extreme. We are changed, and for the better.

It's my hope you will get as much enjoyment out of reading these jokes as I did when putting them together for all of us.

Note:
Unlike most traditional books, this one is written and presented in a kind of stand-up comedy style. A wonderful variety of great jokes and rib-tickling humor are all mixed together with great quotes, so that you don't know what to expect next. (And a lot less organizing for me.) So, cast aside your expectations for a table of contents and plunge into a barrel of laughs.

But first:
One day I got talking to a nice homeless lady in the Bagel Nosh café in Santa Monica Ca. As we were swopping jokes she shared this delightful and little-known limerick-poem with me. She will be delighted to know I can now share it with you .

Imagine !

It was early in December as I very well remember
I was walking down the street in drunken pride
But my feet were all a flutter and I landed in the gutter
And a pig came and lay down by my side
As I lay there in the gutter thinking thoughts I could
not utter a colleen passing by did softly say
You can tell a man is cheap by the company he keeps
With that the pig got up and walked away.

A guy goes into the doctor's office and says: I've broken my leg in three places. Doctor says: Well, stop going to those places.

A man runs into the doctors office saying:
Doctor there is an invisible man outside who says he wants to talk to you. What should I tell him?
Doctor says: Tell him I can't see him today.

Murphy was to make his first parachute jump:
It's easy, his friend said. Jump out, count to 10, shout Geronimo and then pull the cord. You'll be fine.
Murphy jumps out but his parachute does not open and he crashes through some trees to the ground. His friend runs over:
What happened?
Looking up, Murphy says: What was the name of that darn Indian fella again?

Did you hear what happened the helpless bachelor when he tried to iron his shirt? He burnt his chest.

Two men drinking in a bar: One says: Gee! My wife's an angel. The other says: You're lucky, mine's still alive.

The father was questioning his daughter's fiancee: Young man are you able to support a family? Well sir, he replied, I was just planning to support your daughter; the rest of you will have to fend for yourselves.

When I was traveling long distance last week, I picked up a hitch-hiker. But you kinda have to when you hit them.

It is Christmas time as I write this and my younger brother in Ireland emailed me this salutary warning on the dangers of drinking and driving.
He said: Everyone should read this written by my friend Mark.
From Mark: I went out to a Christmas party last week and, unfortunately, I had a few drinks too many. I decided to take the bus home. I arrived there safe and sound, which is quite remarkable, because I have never driven a bus before and I have no idea where I got it.

Man to chef in roadside Diner:
I'd like two watery eggs, three slimy pieces of bacon, some burnt toast and a cold cup of coffee, please.
Chef: You're having me on; I can't give you that.
Man: You did yesterday morning.

Patient: I have this terrible problem; I'm always telling lies. Psychiatrist: I don't believe you.

I was in the bar last Saturday night knocking back a few drinks and there were two very large women there; they both had pretty strong accents so I said: Hey, are you two ladies from Ireland?

One chirped up: Wales, you stupid idiot so I apologized, I said: I'm very sorry. Are you two whales from Ireland?
A man sticks his head into an igloo and asks: Any blubber here?
The Eskimo replies: No blubbers, two sisters.

The friendly, honest, social man, tis' he who fills great nature's plan, 'tis he and only he.

My doctor said I only had six months left to live. I went back to tell him that I wouldn't be able to pay his bill so he gave me another six months.

Heard at bar: My ex-wife still misses me but her aim is getting better.

Did you hear about the man with two wooden legs whose house caught on fire? The firemen managed to save his house but he was burnt to the ground.

In Sheffield, England back in the 1940's they'd never hang a man with a wooden leg. They said they needed a rope.

Hard drinking Brennan went to the doctor with stomach pains. After examining him, for quite a while, the doctor says: I don't seem to be able to find anything wrong with you; I'll have to put it down to drink.
Ah! That's ok doctor, said Murphy, I'll come back some day when you're sober.

I have a neighbor who has a brake fluid addiction but he says he can stop anytime and his brother is addicted to soap but he says he's clean
I'm working on a joke about mountain climbing but I haven't made it up yet. And my joke about unemployment just isn't working.

A woman gets on a bus with her baby.

The driver says: Ugh! That's got to be the ugliest baby I've ever seen in my entire life!
The furious woman goes to the back of the bus. A kind man asks her what's the matter. She says, That bus driver just insulted me.
The man says: Well, don't let him away with it; just go up there and tell him off. Give him a piece of your mind. Go now, I'll hold your monkey for you.

Life is progress from want to want not from enjoyment to enjoyment.

Do you know why you never see a blind man sky dive?
Because it's hard on the dog. (It's a good one)

Psychiatrist: How are you?
Patient: Not too good. I'm feeling really low and depressed. I just can't seem to cheer myself up. What can I do?
Psychiatrist: I have an idea. Why don't you do something different for a change?
Patient: Like what?
Well, why not go to the circus and just enjoy Coco the clown.
Patient: I am Coco the clown.

Did you hear about the insomniac, atheist, dyslexic? He was up all night trying to figure out if there is a dog.

Some days I wake up grumpy. Other days, I just leave her there.

John had been married nearly 50 years. When asked the secret of his long-lasting marriage he surprised everyone by saying: That's easy! On our 20th wedding anniversary I took my wife to Hawaii and on our 45th wedding anniversary, I went and picked her up again.

Better a little with virtue than a large income with injustice.

Guy says: I hate all this terrorist business. I used to love the days when you could see unattended bags or luggage on a bus or train and think to yourself, I could take that.

Sullivan is a nice simple guy. He goes to his fiancée's father and says: I'd like to marry your daughter.
The father says: Have you seen (i.e. spoken to) her mother?
Sullivan: I have. But I prefer to marry your daughter.

A man is walking down the street with a fierce looking dog on a leash: Where are you taking your dog, a man asks.
I'm taking him to the dog-pound to have him put down.
Oh my goodness, the man says; is he mad?
He's not a bit pleased, says the owner.
('Fierce' looking dog alright -:))

Judge at murder trial: But Madame, I'm curious, why did you shoot your husband with a bow and arrow?
Wife: I didn't want to wake the children.

There's nought so queer as folk.

Frank: Maggie, would you brew me some coffee?
Maggie: Why don't you do it yourself Frank, I'm busy.
Frank: But that's women's work.
Maggie: Don't be silly.
After arguing whether he or she should brew the coffee, Maggie had an idea: Let's see if my Bible has anything to say about this. She checks and exclaims: I'm right! Look, it says it right here-Hebrews.

There was a young Scot named Dave who stashed all his cash in a cave. He knew all too well of the 'Banksters' cartel and was proud of the money he saved.

I went into a bar in Scotland and the barman said: What would you like to drink sir? Scotch on the rocks, please, I said.
Certainly sir he said and then he threw Angus McGregor over a cliff.
(I wasn't expecting that.)

Guy in coffee shop: How much for a coffee? $1. 75 How much for a refill? Refills are free. Ok, just give me a refill then.

How do you know that a hippie has been sleeping on your couch? He's still there.

Why the little girl laughed at her overworked mother's demand who said; Just don't do something sit there.

I bought a wooden whistle but it wouldn't whistle ; then I bought a steel whistle but it steel wouldn't whistle; then finally I bought a tin whistle and it <u>tin</u> whistle. My parents thought I was a problem child so they sent me to this child- psychiatrist but the kid didn't do me a bit of good.

A time when life was harder but simpler.
In the background, the beautiful, celebrated in song,
"Mountains of Mourne that sweep down to the sea."
Where we spent our childhood summers.

Man in barber shop in Galway Ireland.
I want my hair cut like Tom Cruise.
Big rough barber says: Sit down.
He cuts his hair, and then proceeds to shave him bald.
The man looks in the mirror and complains: Hey! Tom Cruise doesn't have his hair cut like this.
Big rough barber says: He does if he comes in here.

A man was curious as he observed four look-a-like, long-haired female hippies. He approached them and said: Are you sisters?
No! One of them replied; we're not even catholic.

Judge to thief: Why is it that all your robberies have been on the third floor of different five story buildings?
Thief: Well, that's my story and I'm sticking to it.

My great grandfather's was an 1898 marriage; she was 18 and he was 98. (Not really)

A man of conscience is one who never acquires tolerance, well-being, success, public standing and approval on the part of prevailing opinion at the expense of truth.

Each day of our lives we march closer to our date with destiny.

Stranded on a deserted island Harry was granted two wishes by a genie he had accidentally stumbled upon.

His first wish: A cold glass of Guinness beer that would never empty, just keep refilling itself, was instantly granted.
He drank it slowly then sat it down. It immediately filled up.
Now what is your second wish? The genie asked.
He said: I'll have the same again.

The Four Last Things:
Death, Judgment, Heaven or Hell.

A married couple, both 60 years of age, stumbled across a genie who granted each of them one wish.
The wife says: I would love to spend the summer with my children on the east coast.
The genie grants her wish, and off she goes.
The genie then says: What is your wish, good sir. Husband: I've often wished that my wife were 30 years younger than me. The genie says: Your wish has been granted sir. You are now 90 years of (A genie with a sense of humor.) What lies at the bottom of the sea and twitches?
A nervous wreck.

Seven brides for seven brothers?
I suspect that waiting for the bathroom is probably where they learned to dance so well.

Airport Security guard: What's in that bag that you are carrying over your shoulder? Man says: Ducks. How many ducks? Man answers: If you guess right I'll give you all three.

Well-known drinker, Murphy, appears before the exasperated judge.
Judge says: Murphy! You were brought in here again last night between two policemen; drunk I suppose?
Murphy: Yes, your honor, they were, the both of them.

Seamus was always looking for bargains: The salesman says: Can I help you sir? Seamus responds: Could I speak to the manager please? The manager appears and says: Can I help you sir? Seamus: Hi! Yes, could you, please, show me the cheapest suit you have in the store? The manager looks him up and down and says: You're wearing it sir.

Teacher; Now tell me honestly Simon, do you say prayers before eating your meals? Simon: No, we don't have to, our mom's a good cook.

Absolute truth is a reality: "He who makes himself his own teacher becomes the pupil of a fool. We should be humble enough to be taught by God through men."
False tolerance.
Tolerance does not mean avoiding differences on the ground that there is "your truth" and "my truth" but nothing that both of us could ever recognize as the truth.

The ship's captain calls the First Mate; I just got the news that Kavolskie's mother died. Please inform him, but be more tactful and don't just blurt it out like you did the last time you brought a crew member bad news. That guy was in shock for weeks.
Yes sir; certainly sir. I will; I'll think of something appropriate. Trust me. Through the loud speakers he calls. All hands on deck, all hands on deck. They rush to line up at attention:
First mate: I want you to listen carefully. Now, I want all of you who have mothers who are still alive to take one step forward – not so fast Kavolskie.

When the Apple computer genius, Steve Jobs, died and went to heaven he was stunned, bewildered, in fact, at the great welcome he received with everyone there to greet him with beautiful music. All of heaven was there. God-the-Father explained:
You have to understand, Steve, that we haven't had this much excitement here in heaven over an apple since Adam and Eve.

Laugh and the World Laughs with You...

Two men, poking around in an attic, found an old ticket for a pair of shoes that had been left in for repair nearly ten years before. Curious, they proceeded to the nearby shoe-repair shop and presented the ticket. The owner rummaged around for a while in the back of the shop. He came out and handed them back the ticket and said: They'll be ready on Wednesday.

Buddhist: You have got to be the most thoughtless person I have ever met in my entire life.
Pupil: Thank you Master.

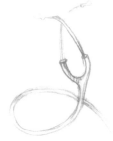

Buddhist receives a birthday greeting from his very best friend which reads: Not thinking of you on your birthday.

A renowned doctor is being shown around the grounds of an elderly nursing home.
He sees a guy walking in the road, holding his arms out in front, as if holding a steering wheel – he proceeds to simulate changing gears and all the while making car noises.
What's wrong with him? The doctor asks.
Oh, he thinks he's in a car, racing.
Doctor: I think I understand the problem. I can cure that.
Oh no – you can't do that.
Why not? The doctor asks.
Because he pays me $20 to clean it.

A man may imagine he understands something but still not understand anything as he ought.

In wartime Frank and Maggie were running up the street heading for the hills, to escape the bombings.
Maggie suddenly stopped. What's the matter Maggie? Frank asks.
Maggie says: Oh, I forgot my teeth.
Frank says: For God's sake Maggie, its bombs they're dropping, not sandwiches!

A man looking in a pet shop for a bird that could sing found one in the corner. I'll take this one, he said; it sings great. Owner: Would you bring him over to me, please? As the customer goes to take it out of the cage he sees that the parrot has only one leg. Hey! He complains to the owner, this parrot has only got one leg. Well, make up your mind, says the owner; is it a singer or a dancer you want?

Gary would never go on a vacation, as he could not bear to leave his beloved cat. His friend George assured him he would take good care of the cat in his absence, so he relented and went off to France.
A week later the friend calls Gary and says: Your cat is dead.
Gentle Gary really loved his cat and he was in a state of shock for several days. Later he called his friend to reprimand him: You don't break bad news like that – like a crack of thunder out of a clear blue sky!
Well, what should I have said? His friend asked.
Well, you could have started by saying that the cat was up on the roof and wouldn't come down; then the next day you could have called and said that it fell off the roof and was at the vet's hospital. Then you could have called me later and told me how it didn't look good and finally, that he had died. It would have been a lot kinder. That way I would at least be prepared. Sorry about that, said his friend.
One week later, Gary answers the phone again. It's his friend:
Gary said: What is it this time?
Friend: Well Gary, it's your mother. I'm calling to tell you that she's up on the roof....
You can't decide what's right by what's popular, especially if it is a media-driven popularity.

Sally, does this dress make me look fat?
No Shelia; it's all that pasta and ice cream you eat that is to blame.

Master of Ceremonies at a Convention: Now our next speaker needs no introduction; he's not coming. He got a better offer.

If at first you don't succeed skydiving is not for you.

Steak and kidney pie is a popular dish in England, as are fish and chips:
Waiter: What would you like to order sir?
Customer: I'd like some steak and kiddlee pie.
Waiter: Pardon?
Customer: Steak and kiddlee pie, please.
Waiter: Oh, you mean steak and <u>kidney</u> pie?
Customer: That's what I said, diddle-I?

What do sea monsters eat?
Fish and ships.

One shopper to another at the meat counter:
You've really got to wonder what kind of disease that cured ham might have had.

Conscience is at the service of truth and truth does violence to no one.
....

First Confession: In preparing the children for their first confession, one boy asked the priest: Fr. Kevin, you know how we say that this is our first confession. Does that mean, sometimes there will be a second confession? (Good question.)
.... The doctor comes out to the anxious patient to give him his test results.
It's good news Mr. Jones; it's not hypochondria, you really are as ill as you think. (Some doctor.)

Did you hear about the cross-eyed teacher who was fired? She couldn't control her pupils.

O'Rourke had saved up his money and gone off for three weeks for a great vacation, on the Continent. He was only back a week when he dropped dead. At the wake, in his home, Mrs. Mc Cann and her friend were examining him in the coffin. I've never seen him looking better, she said. That vacation must have done him a world of good.

Actual courtroom exchange:
Q. Do you recall the time you examined the body?
A. Yes! The autopsy started at around 8. 30 pm.
Q. And Mr. Doran was dead, at that time?
A. No, he was sitting up on the table, wondering why I was doing an autopsy.

Nothing more difficult and therefore more precious than to be able to decide.

Did you know that a lot of women these days are becoming Mormons? Yes! They figure, the Mormen the better.
(Try it out verbally. Mormons like it too.)

At an exam center:
Examiner to pupil: Now, realize that our next test is an oral test. That means that all your answers must be oral. First: What is your date of birth?
Student: Oral.

After an argument the wife says:
I was a fool when I married you.
Husband: Yes dear, but I was in love then and didn't notice.

Father to son: Actually, there are three rings in life: The engagement ring, the wedding ring and suffering.

Great spirits often encounter violent opposition from those of mediocre minds.

The phone rings in the hospital.
Man says: I'm enquiring about Patrick Brennan.

Nurse: I will put you through to the nurse in charge. The nurse answers.
Man: I'm enquiring about Patrick Brennan, how is he doing? Nurse: Oh yes, he's doing great. He should be out of here in about a week. Can I tell him whose calling?
Man: This <u>is</u> Patrick Brennan, the doctor tells <u>me</u> nothing.

The reason every nurse must always carry a red pen is so that they can draw blood.

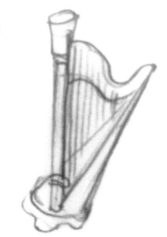

Teacher to her grammar class: Consider this sentence:
Don't have no fun at the weekend.
Now, how would I correct that ? she asked.
Student: Try and find a boyfriend.

Irish Lass to her host for the evening:
Gosh Seamus, I've had enough fun tonight to last me ten years.
See ya then, he says.

Did you hear the one About the...

Do you know the three financial reasons why a duck should enter water?
    To float a loan
    To liquidate a bill
    To go to the bank and make a small deposit.

Why do witches wear name tags?
Witches wear name tags so each witch will know which witch is which.

A man buys a lottery ticket and wins. He calls his wife and says:
Honey! I won the lottery, pack your bags.
Wife – all excited: Where are we going?
Husband replies: I don't know but be out of the house by the time I get home. (Yes! Cruel.)
Oh death, where is your victory, where is your sting?
The ailing Robin Hood on his death-bed, makes a last request:
Friar Tuck, please bring me my trusty bow and arrow. Open the window, please, so that I can gaze on my beloved Sherwood Forrest one last time. Wherever my faithful arrow shall land there also I wish to be buried.
So they buried him on top of the closet.

Two fish in a tank; one says to the other: How the heck do you drive this thing?

Two fish swimming hit a brick wall. One says: Dam.

Humanity as a whole and Christians in particular feel the pressing need to give sense and purpose to a world which is increasingly complicated and difficult to be happy in.

Anyone can be a winner if they try hard enough, unless of course, there is a second entry.

If at first you don't succeed skydiving is not for you.

The Baptist parishioner was not coming to Church and when asked why not by his caring pastor, he explained: I'm embarrassed; I just don't have any nice clothes to dress up in. The kind pastor bought him a whole new wardrobe of clothes but he still did not come to church. Calling on him again the Baptist pastor asked why. 'Man says: Well, to tell you the truth, Reverend, I looked so good in the new clothes that I decided to become a Presbyterian.

Fr. Murphy stood up in the Pulpit preaching his hell-fire and brimstone sermon. It was the men's annual Retreat and he had everyone scared stiff. Now, he said I want everyone here who wants to go to heaven to stand up. The entire congregation stood up. Sit down, he said. They all sat down. Now I want anyone here who wants to go to hell to stand up. Everyone remained seated, of course-except Flanagan, right there in the middle of the church. Fr. Murphy glared at him; do you mean to tell me, Flanagan, that you want to go to hell?
Murphy: No, Father, but I didn't like ta see ya standin' there all by yerself.

Son to his miser father: Dad, could you lend me a hundred dollars?
Miser says: Fifty dollars? What does a young man like you want with thirty dollars?

On the night before his wedding his Best Man tells the Groom:
I believe that a man is incomplete until he's married.
Groom: That's nice. Thanks.
Best man continuing: then he's really finished!

Most men lead lives of quiet desperation. Most men go to their graves with their music still in them.

What did your husband say before he died ? the detective asked. Wife: He just put his hands across his chest like this and then he fell backwards.
No, I mean did he say anything – words, I mean?
Yes, he said: Honey, please don't pull the trigger.

A pickpocket (from force of habit) during confession, managed to steal the priest's wrist- watch but had instant remorse.
Pickpocket: Bless me Father; I stole an expensive wristwatch. Priest: Well, you know my son that you must return it to the owner.
Pickpocket: Here, you take it, Father?
Priest: Oh no, my son, you must return it to the owner.
Pickpocket: I tried, Father, to give it back but the owner doesn't want it.
Priest: Oh well, in that case my son, you keep it.

On returning home from their Sunday church service, the wife says to her husband:
Frank, did you see that Maggie Maguire one, up there in front of us in church? Her, with her big fancy coat, her new hair-do and her pearl ear-rings? Just who does she think she is?
No, I can't say I did, said Frank.
Wife: Oh well, a fat lot of good going to church does you.

A lie has a certain attraction to those who wish to believe it.

Woman in court charged with assaulting Paddy Muldoon:
Judge: Maggie Feeney, the evidence proves that you threw a brick at this, here present, Paddy Muldoon.
Maggie: The evidence proves more than that judge; it proves I hit him.

Dialogue between Military Doctor and new recruit:
Doctor: How are your bowels working?
Recruit: Haven't been issued with any, sir.
Doctor: I mean, are you constipated?
Recruit: No, I volunteered.
Doctor: Heavens man, don't you know the King's-English?
Recruit: No sir. Is he?

Lady: I've told my husband that if I die before him I want to be buried at the golf course. That way I know he'll come and see me four or five times a week.

Of all the gin joints in all the towns, in all the world, she had to walk into mine.

The gentle old rabbi was at his wits end over his parrot's bad language.
A kind neighbor had an idea.
I have a female parrot, she said, who is a little saint and who's only words, all day long, are: Let us pray. Let's see if her good example can reform him.
She brought the offending parrot home with her. As soon as he was placed in the cage with the lady parrot he took one look at her and said: Hi ya sweetie, how about a kiss?
She smiled sweetly at him and said: My prayers have been answered.

President of company: I was told that you could you give me a reference for this man, Patrick Walsh? Will you vouch for him?
Oh, yes indeed. He's great. I can assure you that his character is beyond reproach. You just have to watch out for him a little bit. You know- keep an eye on him.
(Some reference!)

A villager could see in the distance a man on a donkey coming towards him. As they got closer he could see that a woman was walking along side and holding on to the donkey. Curious, the man stopped them and said: I see that you are up there riding on the donkey and your wife is down here walking. Why is <u>she</u> walking?
'Cause she doesn't have a donkey, he replied.

Native American is lying on the road with his ear glued to the ground.

One of the townsfolk says: Oh! I suppose you are listening to see when the stagecoach is coming by?
Native American: Stagecoach already come by – 'ran over my neck.

The friendly, honest, social man; 'tis he who fills great nature's plan, 'tis he and only he.

Parrot perched at entrance to a pet shop:
An overweight lady walks by and the parrot says: You're fat and you're ugly
The next day the same thing: You're fat and you're ugly. Again the third day: You're fat and you're ugly.
The woman had had enough and marched into the shop and complained to the manager.
He consoled her. Oh, I'm very sorry. I can assure you it will not happen again.
Sure enough, the next day as she approached, she could see that the parrot had his head down and was very quiet. But as she passed by, he looked up and said: You know!

Religion is not a sideshow but central to ones fulfillment in this life and ultimate happiness in eternity.

Two eggs boiling in a pot; one says to the other: Gee! It's hot in here.
The other says; this is nothing; wait until you get outside, they bash your head in.

Guy comes running into the doctor's office:
Doctor, doctor I have only three minutes left to live; is there something you can do for me?
Doctor says: Well, I could boil you an egg.

Two men on a park bench:
Nice man to his down-and-out, sad-faced companion:
Hey Fred! Would you like to come over tonight for a little Christmas party? Fred: You're not inviting me out of pity, are you?
No, of course not.
Fred: Too bad; I was hoping for a little pity.
(It happens.)

Buddha's conversation with a New York hot dog vendor:
Vendor: What do you want on your hotdog?
Buddha: Oh, just make me one with everything!
Vendor: Ha! As long as you don't relish in it.
Buddha: Very funny. Now, could I have my change please?
Vendor: Oh Buddha, you of all people should know change comes from within.
Buddha: Listen I may be a pacifist, but if you don't give me back my change I may have to pass-my-fist across your face.

When the heart speaks, other hearts must listen.

The ventriloquist's dummy was making all these derogatory jokes about "….dumb Kerry-men."
(Kerry is one of the greatest of the thirty-two counties of Ireland.)
A man in the audience stood up to complain: Look, I'm a Kerry-man and I strongly object to all these dumb Kerry-men jokes.
I'm sorry sir, said the ventriloquist, we mean no harm. Nobody <u>really</u> believes that Kerry-men are stupid.
Kerry-man: I'm not talking to YOU; I'm talking to that little git on your knee!"

The average male gets his living by such depressing devices that boredom becomes a natural state to him.

Paddy decided to raffle off his donkey, as he needed some money. After he had sold about two hundred tickets, at two euros each, his donkey died. Oh, what am I going to do now? I know! I'll call up the winner and give him back his two euros.

Every time you smile at someone, it is an action of love, a gift to that person, a beautiful thing.

Dialogue with Bogart, in Casablanca movie:
You despise me, don't you? said the thief.
Bogart: Well! I suppose if I ever gave you a thought, I guess I would.

At Christmas time, Mary was rewarded for being good with a big stocking full of goodies, with a gold watch on top.
Patrick, who had been very bad (and to teach him a lesson) had his stocking filled with horse manure.
On Christmas morning Mary says:
Oh look, Patrick, I have a watch (She puts it to her ear :.) and it's going.
Patrick, looking into his stocking quips: That's nothing, Mary. I have a horse and it's gone.

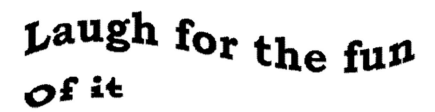

Did you ever wonder what makes the Leaning tower of Pisa lean?
It never eats.

The Mother Superior nun was dying and could take nothing to drink but milk. Even that she did not like. Out of compassion her nun friend started, secretly, to add whiskey to the milk. The dying woman loved it. This continued for some weeks until death itself claimed her. Her last words to her fellow sister nuns surprised them: Whatever you do, don't kill the cow.

Two old-timers are watching a beautiful, curvaceous young woman walking on the other side of the street and one says: Do you know, there was a time when that would have done something for me – but I can't for the life of me remember what it was.

If it's true: Tis' better to have loved and lost than never to have loved at all, then maybe 'tis better to have loved a short than never to have loved a tall.

A man's life is worth more than the worst thing he ever did.

An atheist, being pursued by a giant bear, found that he had nowhere else to run to and so he turned to face the bear; it too had stopped and was now licking its chops. In fright the man says: God, it would be hypocritical of me, after all these years of ignoring you, to now suddenly start praying to you as Christian would but maybe if you will convert this bear into a Christian I'll be safe.
To his great joy the bear immediately fell to its knees and clasping its paws together in prayer it began to pray out loud;
Bless us o Lord for these thy gifts which we are about to receive…
(Too late now buddy.)

Gems from a cocky English football manager:

England's greatest soccer manager Brian Clough, when asked how he deals with disgruntled players.

Well, if I had an argument with a player, we would sit down for about twenty minutes, talk about it, and then decide I was right.

Other comments by him:

Most people don't have the courage of my convictions.
Reporter: Do you think of yourself as the best ever soccer Manager?
Brian Clough: No I wouldn't say that I'm was the best manger ever but I'm in the top ONE. (Good one!)

That which we do for ourselves will perish miserably, that which we do for others out of love for God, will go on re-echoing throughout all eternity.

Same Football Manager's Reactions to a pesky press reporter:

Reporter welcoming him to a new club and their struggling team: Do you think you are the right man to turn things around for this club?
Rather peeved Manager: No, when I was asked if I thought I was the right man for the job I said, No, I think you should have got someone else because I'm bloody useless. Of course I think I am the right man.   (Reporters loved his wit)

The same annoying reporter, after a win, to the same manager: You must be delighted with that result?
Manager: You're spot on! You can read me like a book. We <u>won.</u> 'Course I'm delighted.

She sells sea shells by the sea shore.

Reporter to Manager after a defeat:

Bang, there goes your unbeaten run. Can you take it?
Manager: No, I'm just going to crumble like a wreck. I'll go home, become an alcoholic and maybe jump off a bridge. Umm, I think I can take it, yeah!
Reporter: There's no negative vibes or negative feelings here?
Manager, who had had enough of these dumb questions answered: Apart from yourself, we're all quite positive around here. I'm going to whack you over the head with a big stick. Down negative man, down.

Same manager- to a recently signed (at great expense) player who was performing really poorly:
Have you bought a house in town yet?
Player: No boss, I have not.
Manager: Well don't bother.

To a player he who was considering moving to a different club:
My advice is to ignore the thought that the grass is greener elsewhere because you might find when you get there that the cows have crapped on it.

Why do cows have no money?
Because people milk them dry.

(This manager, Brian Clough, is the only English league manager to have won two European Cup soccer titles. Must have been fun to play for him.)

We will walk down that path to forever, naked and alone, with no props, prompters, stand-ins or excuses, no one but ourselves to blame for our sins.

Pastor: Frank, you've been married happily for fifty years; what's your secret?
You see, I want to give a young couple some good advice. Is there any one thing in particular that helps you to be so successful?
Frank: Yes! There is. All our married life Maggie and I have gone out to eat twice a week. Maggie goes on Mondays and I go on Saturdays.

In Personal column: Young professional lady seeks rich, elderly gentleman, in poor health, with a view to lasting relationship. (With his money?)

Friend: So you really think he's a very good man, a man of real integrity?
Mark Twain: Yes, certainly ! But fewer things are harder to put up with than the annoyance of good example.

Chance favors the prepared mind.

The silent monks would take turns once a year to speak only one sentence to the rest of the monks:
The 1st year, the 1st monk says: I hate porridge.
The 2nd year, the 2nd monk says: I love porridge.
The 3rd year, the 3rd monk says: I wish you two guys would stop quarreling.

The old missionary was very nervous as he had never preached to a tribe of Native American Indian chiefs before. He was pleasantly surprised when they really got enthusiastic, even shouting "Gumba! Gumba!" at times, especially when he would make a new interesting point.
Afterwards he was telling his host: That was very edifying; I don't usually get that kind of passionate response. It was getting late so, as he was leaving the host called out to him: Be careful there, Reverend, when you're crossing the cow field, that you don't step in the gumba.

College Student: Hey, Dad! I've got some great news for you.
Father: What, son?
Son: Remember that $500 you promised me if I made the Dean's list?
Father: I certainly do.
Son: Well, you get to keep it.

I don't buy what the saints all say because according to them I'm better than they.

At the television awards ceremony one winner was humble enough to say: The people, truly responsible for my success are my four writers. Following him to the winner's podium was a well-known and popular Christian preacher:
I, also, want to thank my four writers - Matthew, Mark, Luke and John.

Time Management Study Report:
Indecision may or may not be the problem here. (worth the money? No.)

Peeved mother's note to teacher: Please Miss; will you let my wee lad go to the toilet when he wants to, not when you want?

Teacher, in Art Class:
Sarah, what are you drawing?
Little Sarah: I'm drawing a picture of God
Teacher: But Sarah, no one knows what God looks like.

Little Sarah kept on drawing and answered: They will in a minute.

And where you find no love, put love, and you will find love.

Teacher: Johnny, why were you not at school yesterday?
Johnny: Ah, my uncle got burnt.
Teacher: Was he badly burned?
Johnny: Ah, sure you know, they don't muck around with them cremations.

Paddy in confession: I have to confess Father; I know I'm such a handsome, desirable man. In fact, I do believe that I am probably the best catch -- the most eligible man in the entire county. So, it's a terrible sin of pride- I must confess.
Priest: No Paddy, relax! That's not a sin of pride; that's just a mistake?

Why did the feminist cross the road?
Why shouldn't she!

So you're off to <u>another</u> funeral Sammy?
Sammy: Yes, I am. I believe that you should always go to other people's funerals because if you don't go to theirs, they won't come to yours.

Every time a man stands up for an idea or acts to improve the lot of others, or strikes out against injustice, he sends forth a tiny ripple of hope....

The villagers decided to break into Dracula's castle and put an end to him. They arrived, armed with a hammer and a stake. And, sure enough, there he was, lying in the coffin. Gustav, the blacksmith, raised his hammer- ready to drive the stake through his heart but stopped, looked down and asked: How would you like your stake Dracula? (Funny guy)

Detective: I wonder if Randy could help us in our search.
Deputy: Ah! No; Randy couldn't help us find anything. He's hopeless!
Randy couldn't even find a prayer in the Bible

How's your dad doing since he lost his job?
Rita: Not good. Yesterday I heard him tell someone that he's so poor now that he has to borrow money to buy water to cry with.

Mr. Jones, when driving long distance, was pulled over by a motor-cycle cop who said: Your wife fell out of the car five miles back. I've been chasing you down all this time.
Jones: Oh, thanks be to God Officer. I was starting to think my hearing had gone.

Excuse me; I'm doing a survey on self-defense. Would you know how to defend yourself against a karate attack?
Man: No, I'm afraid I wouldn't.
Good! Give me your wallet.

Psychiatrist: What kind of a father was your dad?
Troubled businessman's answer: Well, my dad had a profound influence on me; he was a lunatic.

It is a beautiful thing when you come to know that there is more to you than yourself. A thing of beauty is a joy forever.

Contagious
The Reverend Brown got an unusual call for help from another district to attend to a very sick person. He obliged. Afterwards he asked: How come you did not call one of your own clergy; are you short-handed?
Oh no, we just didn't know if it was contagious and didn't want to take the chance.

Mc Crackin was the most despised and most hated man in the village. When he died there was no one to go to his funeral.
Out of charity the priest cajoled a dozen or so resistant locals to show up in church for the funeral service.
When he had finished he looked down and enquired: Now is there anyone here who has a good word to say about the deceased before we lay him to his eternal rest?
There was total silence, not a movement.
This is awful, said the priest. 'Call yourselves Christians. He ordered that all the windows and doors of the church be locked down, saying angrily:
Now no one is leaving this church until SOMEONE has a good word to say about this poor soul.
After a pause timid little Flanagan rose up from his seat.
Well Flanagan, said the priest, have you something nice to say about the deceased?
Yes Father, said Flanagan: Well say, it demanded the priest.
Flanagan: His brother was worse.

A small house will hold a hundred friends; the house of the heart is never full.

Hopeless young lady:
I don't know about my psychiatrist. Yesterday he told me that I need to change the tone of my self- deprecating. And the last time I saw him he told me that I should practice denial.

Joe got up to leave his group of friends.
Fred said:
So long, Joe; see you later.
Joe replied: Well, I've had a wonderful time - but this wasn't it.
Fred: You know Joe, come to think of it, some people spread joy and happiness wherever they go; others <u>whenever</u> they go.

Murphy went to the doctor and said to the doctor: what is a good cure for insomnia?
Doctor: A good night's sleep.

Very Irish: O'Toole's car broke down late one winter's night, on a dark country road. He walked to the nearest (but unlit) farm house and after much knocking the owner, from the second floor, pulled up a window and angrily shouted down to him: What do you want?
Looking up Flanagan said: My car broke down; can I stay here for the night?
Yes, said the farmer, and slammed the window shut. (Cold comfort.)

History would be a wonderful thing – if it were only true.

The little Catholic boy said to this little Jewish friend:
Our parish priest knows much more than your rabbi.
The Jewish kid says: Of course he does, because <u>you</u> tell him everything. (Confession.)

Interviewer to applicant:
I have reviewed your application
I found no lies, distortions or exaggerations. In fact, it was all- true. Whatever makes you think that you're qualified for Real Estate?

Flighty lady: I'd like to arrange a date for my wedding.
Pastor: Look Madame, this is your fourth wedding in four years. Don't you realize that religion's not a sideshow and that marriage is a lifelong commitment? It's not just some sort of musical-chairs adventure.

('Actually said by my pastor.)

Sid: 'Haven't seen you for a while, how's your portfolio doing? Anything new?
Fredrick: Well yes! I've learned that with a million dollars and some insider information, one can go broke in a year.

He who laughs Last....

Pat's companion Armand had very bad eating habits. After yet another distressing visit to a restaurant, Pat said: You know Armand, when you went to the bathroom everyone was talking about you. They all said that you are not fit to eat with pigs, but I stood up for you; I defended your good name. I said that you were.

How did the operation go doctor?
Well, the operation was a great success but the patient died.

On his grave stone the hypochondriac had it written: *Now will you believe me?*

A group of lads were hanging around a Belfast street corner when an old lady, passing by said.
That's a cold night to be out lads; would you take a bowl of yesterday's soup?
Yes, sure, they replied. That's very nice of you.
Lady: Will you come back tomorrow?
(Ah! You have to be Irish for that one.)

We throw rocks at a tree that bears fruit. If the tree has no fruit, we bear no interest. A critic is one who leaves no turn unstoned.

Boss to Employee: Mr. Molloy, I really don't know how this company could do without you but starting Monday, we're going to try. (Yeah, thanks a bunch.)

Two women had been out shopping, spending freely.
Over a cup of coffee one was boasting to the other:
You know, it was I who made my husband a millionaire.
Really, said her friend, what was he before you met him?
He was a multi-millionaire.

Mistakes:
The chef covers his mistakes with sauce and gravy.
The builder covers his mistakes with ivy.
The doctor covers his mistakes with clay.

Joe: I told you, John, how my doctor said that he'd have me on my feet in no-time.
John: And did he?
Joe: Yeah! I had to sell my car to pay his bill.

He who would be free, himself must strike the blow.

Mike: Are you happy with your presents Liz?
Luxury-lover Liz: Yes! After all, it's not the thought that counts; it's the gift behind it.

Murphy's wife just had a baby. He called up and enquired how she was doing.
Oh, said the nurse in charge, both mother and child are doing fine.
By the way she said, is this her <u>first</u> child?
No, said Murphy, this is her husband.

Saint Clement was a highly intelligent and witty person but he also had a wicked temper which caused him much embarrassment.
One day he said: I thank God for my bad temper- it shows how fickle and unreliable I

really am. In fact, if it were not for my bad temper I might be tempted to kiss my own hand out of respect for myself.

Courage, the first of human qualities because it is the quality which guarantees all others, but courage needs humility.

Why are you so materialistic? John's friend asked him.
John: Well, I know it's true that money can't buy you happiness, but it can buy you the kind of misery you prefer. And haven't you noticed that when you have money in your pocket, then you are wise, you are handsome, and you sing well, too. (Nothing to be sneezed at, eh?)

A mother could hardly get her son to eat anything at all and was worried about him: My Johnny, she moaned, is so thin that if he stood sideways in school he'd be marked absent.

Life is one long lesson in humility.

A man walking past a cemetery, late one night, hears this tap-tap-tapping noise. Frightened he peers over the wall and sees a man engraving on a tombstone.
He says: You gave me an awful fright; for a minute there I thought you were a ghost.
Reply came: They spelt my name wrong.

Jack's Retirement Dinner speech:
Everything I have today, I owe to the company. Someday, if my conscience bothers me, I may send some of it back.

The local newspaper, commenting on the odd scene of the small town's optician doing cartwheels and summersaults down Main Street: They wrote,
He made a right spectacle of himself.

If I only had a little humility I'd be perfect.

Dirk, the 300 lb. manager of the Unfitness Club is sizing up the frumpy, but relatively slim, 150 lb. female newcomer in front of him:
Look, I'll be honest with you; you're in very good shape, but I think I can help you. We will start you on beanbag chairs with popcorn and eventually move you up to a full size couch with cookies and cokes.

What kind of gun does a vegetarian use? A Ve-gan.

Two trim young ladies in a restaurant:
First woman says: I really like it here.
The other says: I agree, it's a great place to diet - the prices are so high you can't afford to eat.

Tourist in roadside store: Could you tell me, please what is the quickest way to the village?
Farmer: Are you driving or walking?
Tourist: I'm driving. Farmer: Well, sure that's the quickest way.

At the Zoo.
At a time when jobs were scarce, Fred agreed to wear a gorilla suit and act the part of the gorilla that had just died, i.e. until a replacement gorilla could be found.
He enjoyed the job very much and one day in excitement he jumped over into the lion's cage. The lion pounced and ran at him. Fred turned and ran back, screaming: Get me out of here! - Get me out of here!
The lion shouted back: Quiet, you fool, or you'll get us both fired.
The Firing:

Boss: I'm sorry, Frank, we'll have to let you go.
Frank: You know, boss, I never forget a face, but I'll make an exception in your case.

One man with courage makes the majority.

Comedian: When I was born I was so ugly the doctor slapped my mother.

Boss to employee standing with one hand in pocket and his other arm leaning on his push broom:
I know that I asked for a steady worker, but you're absolutely motionless.

An old Irish villager complaining during bad economic times:
Our economy's rotten, we have no proper industry, the weather's desperate and our politicians are idiots but it's a damn fine country to live in just the same. From a prominent Irish tycoon: Our economy's rotten, we have no proper industry, the bottom has fallen out of our agriculture, the weather's desperate and our politicians idiots, but it's a dam fine country to live in all the same.

Typically, his responses were about as illuminating as a candle in the wind.

Ah, Maggie, you're not the girl you used to be.
I wouldn't be too sure of that, says Maggie, there's many a good tune played on an old fiddle. (That's my girl)

Wife to husband: I'd let you talk more, but you're not as interesting as me.

Wife wakes her husband up in the middle of the night.
What's the matter? He asks.
Wife: Oh Frank, I hear a mouse squeaking.
Exasperated husband: What do you want me to do-get up and oil it?

Sloppy Joe is lying, dozing off on the living room couch when his mother walks in with her friend:
Doesn't he have a job? Her friend asks.
His mother says: My son never has a job.
I beg your pardon, says Joe, jumping up; what do you call those things I get fired from all the time?

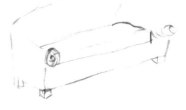

A man flattened by his opponent can get up again and fight on, but a man flattened by conformity will stay down.

Frustrated father to flighty son:
Son, any chance of you finding a job where you can work more than one day a week?

A man in grave yard watches another man weeping by a grave stone and lamenting:
Oh why did you die? Why did you die? Why did you have to die?
The man tries to console him:
You must have loved your wife very much?
He replies: This is not my wife's grave; it's her first husband's.

Overheard at a bar: Marriage is alright, but I think it is carrying love a bit far. (Stay away from that guy)

Patient to Psychiatrist:
Doctor, I sometimes get these weird ideas. What do you mean?
Well, like right now, I feel like I am a pair of curtains.
Psychiatrist: Pull yourself together, man.

A dead fish can go easily with the flow, only a live fish can go against the flow.

Friend: Are you ready to give a talk to our group this afternoon?
Not really! It usually takes me about three weeks to prepare a good impromptu speech.

When the soccer center-forward tried to jump up to head the ball, the defender would jump all over him pushing and hitting him illegally, but the referee, every time, would award a free kick to the offending player - to the consternation of the innocent forward. Commenting on such poor refereeing, the London Observer sports reporter later wrote: It was like penalizing the post-man for illegally thrusting his thigh into the innocent jaws of the terrier.
(I never forgot that. I was at that game. He was spot on.)

Patient: I have this terrible problem.
Psychiatrist: Tell me about it.
Patient: Well! I'm always telling lies.
Psychiatrist: I don't believe you.

Jealousy is the tribute that mediocrity pays to genius.

Straight talking Maggie talking about her neighbor:
He has a face like a well-kept grave. If he died with that face on him, no one would wash him. Sure, I had to tell him the other day: If you're feeling alright would you please notify your face!

I just completed a pleasure trip; I drove my mother-in-law to the airport.

Notice above a car mechanic's messy desk:
Please do not assume that we do not know what we are doing. All items are misplaced exactly where we can find them. Everything is in a well-organized and systematic state of confusion.
(True: I say myself, that a messy desk is a sign of genius).

Questionable ways to acquire a Good Wife:
(Taken from the Bible-Old Testament.)
But still not recommended.
(God has a sense of humor.)
Go to a party and hide. When the women come out to dance, grab one and carry her off to be your wife. (From the Benjaminites Judges 21:19-25)

Find an attractive prisoner of war, bring her home, and shave her head, trim her nails, and give her new clothes. Then she's yours.
That's what it says. (From Deuteronomy 21.11.13)

Best of all: (And maybe hope for all you singles who'd like to be married.) Go out into the field and even if no one is out there, just wander around a bit and you'll definitely find someone. (Cain. Genesis 4:16-17)

It is better to have a permanent income than to be fascinating.

A mother to her hungry, complaining, children:
Just wait; can't you see that I'm preparing dinner as quickly as I can dial?

Doctor: Mrs. Price, your check came back.
Mrs. Price: So did my arthritis. (Good comeback.)

Patient: I keep hearing this ringing in my ear. Psychologist: Don't answer it.

In the driving school car, the bewildered looking gentleman is sitting alone in the car's back seat. In the passenger seat is the driving instructor, pointing and, saying: Remember what you learned yesterday; you've got to sit up here behind the wheel. (That's me and computers)

Sooner or later we have to be at ease with life – we run the show, with no fear of life's negatives, not even death.

An Irish Toast
My God grant that your friends continue to be your friends
May God grant that the hearts of your enemies be turned so that they become your friends
And if he cannot turn their hearts, would He please turn their ankles so you know them by their walk. (Not nice.)

If you don't have anything good to say about anyone, just sit right down here beside me.

There comes an English war dispatch in the desert, which reads: Rommel captured.
Followed immediately by another, which reads: Mistake: Forget that; it should read: Camel ruptured.

Why did they call the elephant Dumbo? That was his name.

We are such stuff as dreams are made of and our little lives are ended with a sleep.

Murphy was praying very hard before the large statue of St. Anthony ("the miracle saint").
I need you to help obtain for me an answer to my problem. Just do your best. I'll be back tomorrow for your answer. Meanwhile, the nuns came by and had to replace the large statue with a little statue of St. Anthony.
When Murphy came back the next day and saw the tiny statue, he said to the smaller St Anthony:
Would you please go back there son and see if your father left me a message?
(Simple faith.)

Psychiatrist: What's the problem?
Patient: It seems that I'm always losing my temper over silly things.
Psychiatrist: Pardon?
Patient: Damn it; I've already told you once.

Do you know what song Eskimos sing at birthdays? You've heard it before; it goes: Freeze a jolly good fellow

The heart has reasons of which reason knows nothing.

Teacher: Does anyone know what a dogma is?
(A binding Article of Faith for Catholics.)
Johnny's answer: Is it a mother of pups?

Teacher: No, but does anyone know what an encyclical is?
(An important Faith document to Catholics.)
Johnny: Isn't it a kind of bicycle that the Pope rides?

Man, with an umbrella hanging from his ear is appealing to a short-sighted man:
Excuse me sir; could you maybe find somewhere else to hang your umbrella?

As if I wasn't self-conscious enough at the way my father would cut my hair (i.e. really severely), my friends would tease me saying:
I like your new haircut; did they give you a bowl of soup with that?

Letter to editor of London newspaper about the government's nation- wide advertising slogan: *Go to work on an egg!*
Dear Editor, I went to work on an egg and it broke down so I took it to a Shell station; they took out the yolk and it goes all white now.

How far that little candle throws its beam, so shines a good deed in a naughty world.

Charlie, the miserably dirty, scruffy, street person is being consoled and encouraged by his friend:

You just have to accept yourself for what you are, Charlie..
Charlie, raising his hand, stops him, saying: Please! I have <u>some</u> standards!

Murphy opened a pub on the moon, but it wasn't very successful. He said there was no atmosphere.

Q: Mr. Murphy, what is your date of birth?
A. September twenty-third
Q. What year?
A. Every year.

If you think yourself generous, measure yourself not by what you give, but by what you hold back.

After a great pep talk by his priest Dominic, a life-long pickpocket, had turned his life around and was now volunteering his services at the local church. Ok Dominic, said the priest (before the Sunday mass), when I say the words Dominus Vobiscum (Latin for: The Lord be with you) that is when you take up the collection and pass the plate around.

When mass was over what a shock for the priest for, as well as the usual envelopes and money, Dominic had also collected wallets, watches, rings, necklaces, passports, purses etc.
What's going on Dominic? The priest asked.
What do you mean Father? As soon as you gave me the signal: "Dominic go frisk-em" I did.

The protestant pastor says to Father Murphy: Have you accepted Jesus Christ as your Lord and savior; have you been saved?
Father Murphy: Well I have but it was a close call and I don't like to talk about it.

Judge: What gear were you in, Madame, when you crashed the car?
Young lady: I believe it was a nice white blouse and black jeans.

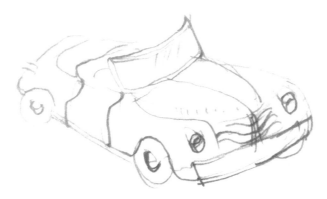

A man was staggering down the street under the weight of a giant grandfather clock. A concerned, elderly gentleman passing him said:
My poor fellow, why don't you carry a wrist watch?

Overheard in a bar:
My neighbor Wilbur really fancies himself as a bit of a wise man. I heard him tell his son the other day: When you come to the fork in the road son, take it.

Brighten your world with laughter...

Wife: Why do you talk so much?
Husband: Well! The only time I am bored is when I'm not speaking.

Villager: What a beautiful autumn day it is, Frank.
84-year-old Frank says: I'll tell you how beautiful it is; it's such a pretty day today that I wish I were working again so that I could take the day off.

Do you know the difference between a recession and a depression? Well! It's a recession when your neighbor loses his job; it's a depression when you lose your own job.

The village pastor was in a panic and he called the Vatican. To his amazement the Pope answered.
I'm sorry to bother you your Holiness.
That's ok, said the Pope; what's the problem?
Pastor: Well, you see, Your Holiness, the good Lord Jesus Christ Himself is walking up the middle of our village. What should I do?
Look busy, said the Pope.

There is a tide in the affairs of men, which, if taken at flood, leads to fortune. If not…. (Regrets.)

Letter from the bank: Dear Mr. Williamson, this is to inform you that our bank profits dropped 40 percent last year and that your account has been debited 25 dollars for this letter. (Isn't that the truth?)

Did you hear what happened to the little boy who ran away with the circus? The police made him give it back again.

What happened
here asked the Police
officer:
Driver: An invisible car came out of nowhere, struck my vehicle and vanished

A lady called her doctor, yet again, late one evening.
Doctor, there is something really wrong with my husband.
Doctor: What do you mean?
Lady: Well, I can be talking to him for hour after hour and he doesn't seem to hear a word of what I am saying. Is it some sort of a disease?
Doctor: No madam, that's not a disease, that's a gift.

He'll regret it until his dying day, if he ever lives that long.

U ngrateful
O'Toole: I heard the great news that your aunt is going to leave you a legacy. Are you pleased?
Murphy: Yeah, but I think that when you have told anyone you have left them a legacy, the only decent thing to do is to die at once.

Customer to travel agent: Are your prices competitive?
Agent: Yes, very much so. Let me put it like this; if anyone goes abroad at a cheaper rate than ours, they've been deported.

After a visit to the restroom the old curmudgeon returned to the doctor's to see that someone had taken his seat.
He grumbled: You wouldn't take my grave so quick.

Admirer: You ask me if she is really that beautiful.
Well, how shall I put it? I would describe her as a tall blonde young woman of such form and dynamism that the tireless waves struggled to get further up the beach just to get closer to her. (Some girl eh?)

Most men lead lives of quiet desperation. Most men go to their graves with their music still in them.

The nurse brings their first-born child to her proud father. He sees the baby smiling and holding out something to him.

The nurse explains: It's a girl and she's got her first credit card.
(You've got to smile!)

I caught a cold in the park. The gate was open.

His people gave the cannibal chief a gift of a large throne to honor him. He was so proud of it he kept it on top of his grass house for all to see. One day it fell and killed him. The moral of the story is: People in grass houses shouldn't stow thrones.

Sullivan, to his friend Seamus: When I die I want you to do something for me.
You know how I love whiskey. Well for forty years I have saved this vintage bottle of whiskey for someone to sprinkle - all of it- over my grave. I want to feel it soak right down into my very bones. Will you do that for me? Will you promise? Just sprinkle it over my grave.
Sure I will my good friend, said Seamus. I'll sprinkle it but is it ok if I drink it first?

Being in a relationship is something that happens to two people who are waiting for something better to come along.

The way we talk in Ireland: Overheard from elderly woman:

Ah doctor, I felt worse many a time when I was half as bad as I am now.

Also: I'll tell you this doctor, I'm as well now as what I was before the way I am now.

Ah dear, sit right down here and have a wee seat; sure the doctor will be with yea in a wee minute.

Three women talking, leaving church and one says: I see our Maggie Magee's wee girl, Trish, is pregnant again. She's getting them rightly. (I heard them say it.)

There is no safety for honest men except by believing all possible evil of evil men.

Do you know why you should never marry a tennis player?
You never marry a tennis player because to a tennis player love means nothing.

Seamus, was watching how another bus passenger was being exceedingly helpful to a foreigner who had just boarded the bus at the airport on a very cold Irish day.
First she had moved over in the crowded bus to

make room for the newcomer, then placed a bag up on the rack for him and then checked to ensure that he was settled- in.

Seamus (who had been entertaining us all about his travels in France), looked over and said to her: You'll be giving him a blanket next.

(I actually witnessed this in Belfast N. Ireland, on the airport bus into the city.)

A doctor, who had stopped to help a man who had collapsed on the sidewalk, after examining him said:
Be quick, we got to get this man to a hospital, right away!
Onlooker: What is it?
Doctor: It's a big tall building with windows

The wife is waiting for her drunk husband to come home in the early hours of the morning. Standing by a tree in the lane she has a white sheet over her head ready to frighten the life out of him and put the fear of God into him.
He cries out: Who's that?
She replies: Tis' the devil.
Oh, he says; thanks be to God. I was afraid it was my wife.

To many, truth is offensive; reason is their enemy.

Fredrick: Do you believe in fairies?
Paddy: Of course not. They do exist just the same.

First man: I like your jacket.
2nd man: Yes but I wish it were a little lighter.
So the first man gave him a lighter and took the jacket.

Curious man to child in check out line:
Excuse me, but are you a little boy or a little girl?
Child: Well, what else could I be?

A little catholic boy and his Jewish friend stopped their play in the park and were arguing over whose religion was the best. Finally the Jewish boy said: Look, we gave <u>you</u> the Ten Commandments.
I know, said the Catholic kid, but we didn't keep them.

Cain became bad because Eve never read anything on child psychology.

Did you ever wonder why nuns wear black? It's just a Habit they get into.

Scoutmaster to two scouts: Did you do your good deed for the day yet?
Yes we did; we took this old lady across the road.
Very good, said the scoutmaster.
Scout: But it wasn't easy;
Why not?
She didn't want to go.

The judge had just finished assessing the amount of fine for drunkenness.
Judge: Well Murphy, its fifty pounds or two weeks in jail. What's it going to be?
Murphy: Oh, I'll take the fifty pounds, sir.

If swimming is good for the figure how do you explain a whale?

In a family of two boys and three girls little Patrick grew up all his life wondering how come his sisters had two brothers and he had only one

Weak men fear strong men, for strong men expose a weak man's weakness.

Smoker: A packet of cigarettes please.
Girl: Large or small?
Small.
Regular or menthol? Regular.
Foreign or domestic? Domestic.
Filtered or unfiltered?
Smoker: Ah! It's ok. I've decided to give them up.

John: You're still not married, Jenny?
Jenny: No! But I want you to know that I'm single by choice; granted, it's my second choice.

Student: Can you teach me to do the splits?
Yoga teacher: How flexible are you?
Student: I can't make Tuesdays.

Seamus: Ok Pat, I'm off to buy the weeks groceries; give me your half of the money.
He returns later with six crates of Guinness beer, two bottles of whiskey and two loaves of bread.
What's going on here? Pat asks.
Seamus says: What do you mean?
Pat says: What's all this bread for?

Man in Fisherman's Wharf Restaurant says to the waitress; do you serve crabs here? Waitress: Just make yourself comfortable, sir; we serve anyone here.

An expert is someone who does everything else worse.

It's quite amazing! When I was in Tokyo I left my watch on a street pole and when I went back a year later it was still there.
The watch was still there?
No! The pole.

Hello, I'm Hawkeye.
Field Sergeant: Oh yes Hawkeye, I've heard a lot about you.
Hawkeye: Well, maybe we can still be friends.

One unhappy employee to an associate:
You know, I deserved that promotion. I was just as under-qualified as the other applicants.

If we have no moral absolutes to guide us, how can we know when we have acted immorally?

Busker: Street–Musician's sign in Galway Ireland: Got no job- Got no car- Got no money - But I'm in a band. (Sounds like my young sons.)

I really wanted to be a tailor but I wasn't suited for it. They said that I wasn't cut out for it.

My lucky number is 5, so on the fifth day of the fifth month
in the year 1995, in the fifth, 5 o clock, race of the day, I put 50 dollars to win on horse number 5 and, wouldn't you know, the darn thing came in fifth.

So, you're Jack. I've heard a lot about you. And it wasn't all bad.

(Nice of you)

Grim death took me without warning; I was well at night and dead in the morning.

Man cannot be separated from God nor politics from morality.

Why it is that film stars are so cool? Because they have so many fans.

Two women coming out of church and one says: That Maggie Mc Conville is an awful holy woman; she's a daily communist. (Overheard in Ireland. She meant communicant-one who receives the holy Eucharist every day.)

Ask and you shall not receive.
When Gus proposed to Kathy she answered:
I know I said I love the simple things in life but I don't want one of them for a husband.

My therapist says I have a preoccupation with vengeance. We'll <u>see</u> about that!

The crowning blessing of life: to be born with a bent to some pursuit.

Why do you avoid Harold so much?
Because he must be ten of the most boring people I know.
What do you call someone with no body and no nose? Nobody nose.

Q. What do you call a camel with 3 humps?
A: Humphrey.

One old enemy to another: You know, I was genuinely sorry that I could not attend your funeral recently.

Heard in court, people explaining their car accidents:

I was sure the old fellow would never make it to the other side of the road when I struck him.

I had been driving my car for forty years when I fell asleep at the wheel and had an accident.

I was thrown from my car as it left the road. I was later found in a ditch by some stray cows.

The guy was all over the road; I had to swerve a number of times before I hit him.

The human proclivity to go beyond the evidence or to ignore it altogether is, unfortunately, widespread.

To avoid hitting the bumper of the car in front, I struck the pedestrian.

The indirect cause of this accident was a little guy in a small car with a big mustache.

I was on my way to the doctors, with rear-end trouble, when my universal joint gave way, causing me to have an accident.

The pedestrian had no idea which way to go so I ran over him.

True it is that men are swayed more by their own sympathies than by honest argument.

I saw the sad face of the slow moving old gentleman as he bounced off the hood of my car.

The telephone pole was approaching fast and I was attempting to swerve out of its path, when it struck my front end.

Officer: How did this accident happen?
Driver: I pulled away from the side of the road, glanced at my mother-in-law and headed over the embankment.

I confess:
Pat had not been to confession for twenty years and was feeling really bad about it.
Pat explained: You see, Father, I work for the lumberyard and every day, for twenty years now, I've been taking wood home for myself without paying for it. Stealing, imagine! Just think Father, every day for twenty years.
The good Father helped him through his confession and for his penance he asked him: Tell me, can you make a novena? (ie. Nine consecutive prayers or actions.) Pat thought for a minute, then said: Well Father, if you have the plans I have the wood

Famous last words:
Witty Oscar Wilde, nearing his death, did not like the wall paper in his room: Either it goes or I go, he said. (The wall paper won.)

Bailiff calls out: The court will now stand for judge Dimbilby (and under his breath added) and if you'll stand for him you'll stand for anything.

Do you know what store I love to shop in most? Said the one-armed man.
A second-hand store.

If you think no one cares if you're dead or alive try missing a few monthly payments.

When I go out to do your work and things just fall apart, give me grace to run to you and hide in your Sacred Heart.

Secretary: How come you have not been returning my calls?
Pastor: So sorry but for the last few weeks I've been busier than a wooden-legged man in a forest fire.

Did you know that statistics show, in the United States, a man gets knocked down every twenty minutes? And he's getting fed-up with it.

Fred: John! Do you have a pen I could borrow?
John: No, sorry!
Fred: Gee John, you know, if there are TWO things I notice you never carry around with you it's a pen.
John: What's the other thing?
Fred: A washing machine. (Well, I think it's funny)

Laughter is the best medicine...

A couple drove down a country road for several miles, not saying a word. An earlier discussion had led to an argument and neither of them wanted to concede their position. As they passed a barnyard of mules, goats and pigs, the husband asked sarcastically, Relatives of yours?
Yep, the wife replied: in-laws.

Fred: Bye John! I got to go now.
John: Ok, I'll see you anon - or a priest.
(A nun or a priest, get it? No? Try some Shakespeare.)

When a man is honest and he hears the truth, he embraces the truth, or he ceases to be honest.

Dear Lord,
Help me to be the kind of person that my dog thinks I am.

Beauty is in the eye of the beer holder.

Definition of a broker: What my broker has made me.

Roses are red, violets are blue; I'm schizophrenic and so am I.

The more honest the man, the less he affects the air of a saint.

Why was the seagull afraid to fly over the bay? He feared it might make him a bagel, then he'd be toast.

Teacher: Cleanliness is next to what?
Billy: Impossible.

Helpful highway signs: Next exit up ahead.
Beware: Locals who have absolutely no idea how to give directions.

Going left at Next Exit up ahead will almost certainly get you hopelessly lost.
Religion teacher: Johnny, would YOU like to go to heaven? Johnny: Yes mame but my mother says I have to go straight home from school.
Clothes maketh the man but it's not the habit that makes the monk.

Horse owner:
I'm at my wits end; I have this great horse which is winning every race, easily, until the home-straight when it suddenly veers off to the left and off the course completely. I've lost six races this way. What can I do?
Trainer: I know what I would do. I would put a piece of lead in its left ear.
How do I do that?
Trainer: With a gun.

Sadly, the elephants were all banned from the swimming pool; they wouldn't keep their trunks up.

Zsa Zsa Gabor: You know, I never hated any of my ex-husbands enough to give them back their jewelry.

Man in library: Fish and chips, please.
Librarian: This is a library.
Oh, sorry, said the man, lowering his voice: Fish and chips, please.

The more things a man is ashamed of, the more respectable he is.

What did the washer say to the thread? Let's fix this nut and bolt.

In a restaurant a young couple were seated at a table not far from an older couple at another table.
It happened that the two women got up at the same time to go to the bathroom.
The young man said: I'll wait here sweetie 'til you get back. He heard the elderly man say to his wife: Honey, I'll go pay the bill and see you at the front door.
He said to the elderly man: That's real nice. After all the years you still call your wife honey.
The elderly man responded: When you get to be my age, son, it's easy. You see, twenty years ago I forgot her name.

Where does Dracula live when he visits New York?
Billy: Oh, I know this one - the Vampire State Building.

Sign on Men's toilet: We aim to please, you aim to please. (Fair enough.)

Oh the gift that God would gee us to see ourselves as others see us.

Teacher: Explain the following words by using them in a sentence.
Some student answers:
Fascinate. John had nine buttons but could only fascinate eight.
Rapture. I rapture parcels.
Office. The man fell office horse.

Dairy. Dairy be late for school again.
Venom. I don't know venom going to town again.
Juicy. Juicy that boy over there?

Comedian: I read in the paper the other day where a dwarf (one of our little people), was pick-pocketed in the streets of London and I couldn't help thinking: What kind of person would stoop so low?

Shouldn't women put pictures of missing husbands on beer cans?

If lawyers are disbarred and clergymen defrocked, doesn't it follow that electricians can be delighted, musicians denoted, cowboys deranged, models deposed (or is it defrocked?), tree surgeons debarked and dry cleaners depressed?

My wife's a treasure; I don't know where I dug her up.

When I was young I was a rather strange child. I used to spend long hours sitting alone reading by the fireside. You see - we didn't have a fireplace.

When a statesman ignores his private conscience in favor of his public duty, he leads his people down the short route to perdition.

I once knew a man with a wooden leg named Pete but I never did get the name of the other leg.

Some traditionally dressed nuns at a baseball game were partially blocking the view of three men behind them. To get a rise out of the nuns the first man, in a loud voice, said:

I'm going to move to Utah, there are only 100 nuns there. The second man said: I'll go to Montana. Only 50 nuns live there. The third man chipped I prefer Idaho. There are only 25 nuns living there.
In the spirit of the occasion one nun-laughing at their antics-turned to them and said: Why don't you all go to hell? There are no nuns there.

If quitters never win and winners never quit, what's all this about, Quit while you're ahead.

Two children talking: Have you ever had chickenpox?
No, I haven't had chickenpox but I have had Chicken McNuggets.

Have you heard about the hump-backed convict who's bent on going straight?

I believe that anyone who runs to a psychiatrist with their problems needs their head examined

Man is not made for defeat. He can be destroyed, but never defeated.

The things children say:
Teacher: Do any of you children have relatives who have been in a war?
Connor: Yes teacher. My uncle Johnny was shot in the ass.
The teacher admonished him:
Rectum, Connor, say rectum.
Connor's response: Rectum! It nearly killed him.

Mary: Do you know why giraffes have such long necks?
Stella: No.
Mary: Because their feet stink. :

Stella. Oh, and I always thought it was just because their heads were so far from their body.

Hard-drinking singer, Dean Martin, used to joke: I once shook hands with Pat Boone (a good Christian singing star) and my whole right side sobered up.

Do you know who the shortest man in the bible is? Answer: Nehemiah. (Knee-hi–miha. Get it?) But it could have been Joshua the shoe-hite.

I went out hunting elephants in my pajamas last night. But don't ask me how the elephants got in my pajamas.

When is medicine is first mentioned in the Bible?
When God gave Moses two tablets.

All that is required for evil to thrive is for good men to do nothing.

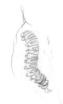 

In the English Literature test the question was: Write down all you know about Yeats.
Student's answer: I don't know anything about Yeats; I don't even know what they are.

First Lady: Guess what Jane? Today I'm getting an expensive set of golf clubs for my husband.
Unhappily married Jane responds:
That sounds like a real good deal to me.

Mother: Johnny, why were you gone so long at the store?
Johnny: I was at the devil's funeral.
Mother: What do you mean? How do you know that?

Johnny: I heard a man say as the funeral got near us, there he goes, the devil himself.

John: Why do you dislike Harold?
Alex: He's a skinflint! Whenever he sees a dollar in another man's hand he takes it as a personal grudge, that is, if he can't take it any other way.

Nervous lawyer to his dentist: Promise me, please, that you will pull the tooth, the whole tooth and nothing but the tooth.

The greatest gain to the whole world is the perfection of one soul.

It was a shock to most of the villagers when rough Jack Bullark was chosen to play the role of Christ in the arduous annual reenactment of the Passion play through the local hill-country. You see, Jack was the most quick-tempered man in the entire village but also the strongest. Many were concerned about his selection, thinking him unworthy. On the Good Friday they were all pleasantly surprised to see how well Jack put up with all the beatings, jeering and taunts aimed at him by those other village actors chosen to be his tormentors. But one wag went too far. He stepped in front of Jack and spat directly into his eye. That was it. Jack had had enough; he was about to drop the cross and have a go at him but stopped himself in time, saying: Ok, Romani, you can have your way now, but just you wait 'til the Resurrection.
(Not quite the Spirit.)

John: What do you get when you cross an elephant with a rhino?
Joe: What?
John: El if I know

One employee, advising the new guy: Be sure you work really hard because, in this firm if you are not fired with enthusiasm you'll be fired with enthusiasm.

Molly at bar: I thought, Claire, that you said you were not going <u>anywhere</u> tonight? Claire: Yes! I didn't <u>want</u> to go out but after I washed my my hair I looked so good, I couldn't very well stay home.

Movie and television producers and writers should create material that shares the human condition and what it means to be a human being. ('rare indeed nowadays. No more Wonderful Life, Casa Blanca writers. We do, though, have Shawshank Redemption's Stephen King.)

God and St Peter are playing golf in heaven.
St. Peter hits his first shot and it lands just off the green. God steps up. He flexes his muscles and takes an almighty swipe at the ball. It sails high and wide towards a wooded area. Just then a seagull catches it in mid-air, in its mouth. He flies back toward the green. The ball then falls out of his beak right on the edge of the green; it rolls about 20 feet towards the hole; it is about to miss the hole by a few inches, when up pops a little worm and knocks the ball into the hole with his head. God is standing there, all pleased with Himself. Not too happy St. Peter goes up to him and says. Come <u>on</u> God! Are we playing golf or are you messin about?

Guess who invented the sewing machine? Some clever sew and sew.

The head psychiatrist is walking on the grounds of the mental institution when an inmate joins him trying to convince the doctor of his sanity, hoping to be released early. I should not be here. I am perfectly normal. Ask me any question you want. When the questions were all answered satisfactorily the doctor agreed: You are right; you are a perfectly normal person and I will put in a good word for your early release at tomorrow's meeting. As he was walking away a brick hit him on the side of the head. Staggering along he looked back and heard the inmate call out. Now, don't forget!

When the British government was taking bids from companies wanting to obtain the contract to build the underground tunnel from England to France one really low bid from Murphy and Sons caught their attention so Murphy and his son were brought in for an interview.

Interviewer: Now, Mr. Murphy, please explain why all the other contractor bids we received for this tunnel job were in the billions of dollars but yours alone is only in the millions?

It's really quite simple said Murphy. We cut out the middle- man.

Really! How come?

Well, you see, I and my lads start at this end and we make our way to France. My son here, with his lads; they start at the other end and head towards England. We all meet in the middle. There's your tunnel.

And what happens if you don't meet in the middle?

Well then, you'll have two tunnels for the price of one. No problem, said Murphy.

My mother-in-law fell down a wishing-well. I never knew they worked.

Good news, bad news.
My mother-in-law drove over a cliff in my new car.

I went on a diet. I swore off drinking and eating dairy products, plus meat and sugar and in fourteen days I lost two weeks.

Sign on wall in Irish police station:
Don't Drink and Drive
Avoid the Mourning After

A lie always has a certain attraction to those who choose to believe it.

Just before the trial was to begin a jury member said to the judge: I cannot, in good conscience, serve as a juror in this case; one look at that defendant convinces me that he is guilty.
Judge: That's the District attorney, madame.

I almost had this beautiful psychic girlfriend when I was twenty, but it was kinda sad because she left me before we met.

Only that which is true can ultimately be loving.

At psychiatrist office: A man is sitting with a trumpet stuffed down the back of his shirt; he has two moose antlers on his head and a small horse shoe dangling from his right ear.
He says to the psychiatrist: I've come to talk to you about my brother.

The aging, whacky, comedian, Phyllis Diller, describing herself: I've had so much plastic surgery that no two parts of my body are the same age. Some say I am the Elizabeth Taylor of the twilight zone. I'm afraid that when I die even God Himself won't recognize me as His child.

Milton Bearl commented.: Her crazy hairstyle makes her look like a leaky Farrah Fawcett. She looks like she was pardoned after the warden threw the switch.
I once went out on a blind date with her, he said; SHE was outdated and I was blind. I should have known. Apparently her previous boyfriend once took her to the Tunnel of Love and told her to wait outside. (What a life.)

My friend has a brake-fluid addiction but he says he can stop anytime.

Little girl: Daddy, why do they call it take-home pay?
Wife interjecting: It's because you can't afford to go anywhere else with it.

When I was a boy, I was told that anybody could become president. I'm beginning to believe it.

Ad in Irish newspaper: Farmers-widow would like to meet a farmer-widower with tractor. Please send photograph of tractor. (A practical woman.)

Teacher: You must have had eggs for breakfast this morning, Bobby.
Bobby: Why do you say that?
Teacher: There is still some egg on your face.
Bobby: Ah no, teacher, that was yesterday's breakfast.

Michael lived to be a healthy one hundred.
When asked how he had managed it, he said to the reporters:
It is quite simple really. Early in my marriage I decided that every time my wife and I had an argument I would go out for a long walk.
I attribute my longevity to the wonderful open-air life I have had. (Me too.)

Alfie says: I had not been to my doctor for a long time. When I walked in he said to me: Hello there, Alfie. I haven't seen you in years, have you been ill or something?

Pay more attention!

Comedian: Whenever my wife asks me the question: Do you notice anything different about me? I know I'm in trouble so now I work from a plan. I start at the floor and work my way up. The other day when she asked just that question I was ready for her. I said: Oh, I see, you bought yourself a new pair of shoes.
Wife: No.
Comedian: Of course, I see now- you bought yourself a lovely dress. It's very nice!
Wife: No.
Comedian: Ah! Yes, you just had a new hair-do. I like it.
No, she hollered; I'm wearing a gas mask.

(Get out of town guy.)

Nothing like a good Laugh...

Do you know why you should be careful about painting people in the nude? Because you <u>could</u> catch cold.

On the other hand - you have different fingers.

Lawyer to judge: Your Honor, we need to reopen my client's case.
Judge: Why?
Lawyer: I've discovered new evidence.
Judge: What sort of evidence?
Lawyer: I've discovered that my client has another ten thousand dollars that I didn't know about until today.

What do you say when you meet a two headed monster? Hello! Hello!

Money won't buy you happiness but it can keep you comfortable while you are being miserable.

The teacher asked the children to complete these sayings and the kid's answered:
    There's none as blind as...Stevie Wonder.
    A penny saved is... not much.
    Two's company three's ...the Musketeers.

When you speak the truth, you don't have to go to great lengths to remember anything.

Overheard in supermarket: Her lawyer is honest but not enough to hurt her case.

The law stated that if during an execution the execution lever failed to work then the prisoner must be set free.

First up was a lawyer and when they pulled the switch it failed. He was let go free. Next up for execution was a doctor. The same thing with him- no electricity. He was set free as well. The executioner was baffled.

Lastly an engineer was up for execution. As he sat there waiting for them to throw the switch he noticed something and said: See that longer wire there, if you move it a little more to the right I think you will find it works fine.

How did our court case go today? inquired the crooked businessman.

Attorney: Well, today, justice has triumphed.
Businessman: Then, there's nothing for it; we'll just have to appeal immediately.

Judge: You two men were caught fighting in the street. What about? Can't this quarrel be settled out of court?
Mulligan: Why, You're Honor, that's what we were trying to do before the police arrived.

Author's mother Maggie RIP. Teacher: What did Washington say to his men before he crossed the Delaware? Student says: Get in the boat?

A homeless person stops a gentleman in the street:
He says: Sir, could you give me a few dollars for a sandwich?
Man says: Certainly! Let me see the sandwich.

A young catholic lady was very much in love with an upstanding young protestant man but would only marry him if he'd agree to become a catholic. He agreed to do so and spent weeks with the local priest diligently learning the Faith. But one catholic teaching really bothered him. He did not like the idea of not being able to eat meat on Fridays and he said so.
Look, said the priest, just keep repeating to yourself. I'm a catholic not a protestant. I'm a catholic not a protestant. That will make it easier on you- just keep saying it, especially on Fridays. Just one week after they were married the priest got a frantic call from the

wife and rushed over to their home. What's wrong he asked? Oh, Father, she cried, come quickly to the kitchen - I think my husband is going mad.

There was the husband with frying pan in hand, leaning over a huge steak and repeating, over and over: You're a fish not a steak- you're a fish not a steak.

Did you hear what happened when the carrot died? There was a big turnip at the funeral. (Groan if you must.)

How many chiropractors does it take to screw in a light bulb? Only one but it will take twelve visits.

What kind of people are never angry? Nomads.

The author's lovely mother Maggie. RIP

Patient: For nearly a year now I've been thinking that I am a fish, not a man.

His psychiatrist had a nice talk with him and gave him some excellent books to read on the subject.
One week later the patient returned, happy as could be, saying: Thanks so much doctor. The books were great; I now see that I am a man not a fish. I won't be needing you anymore. He then left. Seconds later he hurried back in complaining: There's a cat out there and I have no way out.
Psychiatrist; But you know now that you are a man, not a fish? Man says: I know that and you know that but does the cat know that?

If you cannot find contentment within yourself, it is useless to seek it in someone else.

Do you know why barbers in Los Angeles prefer to cut the hair of ten fat men rather than one skinny man?
Because they make ten times as much money. (Makes sense to me.)

Doctor: I'm sorry to have to tell you Joe but your liver is in really bad shape.
Patient: I think, doctor that I'd like a second opinion.
Doctor: Alright then! Your kidney's just as bad.

Jack advised his friend, Hugh, who was always concerned about having no hair on his perfectly bald head:
Hugh, why don't you just get a transplant?
Hugh: Ah, what would I do with a kidney up there?

Be sure never to let your troubles get the better of you. Remember, even Moses was a basket case.

Did you know that God is a great baseball fan?
Yes, the very first words of the bible are: In the big inning.

Two ants were playing soccer in a saucer but the ball kept rolling over the edge.
We'll have to do better than this next week when we play in the cup, one lamented.

The blustery preacher was giving his congregation one of his frequent 'hell -fire and brim-stone' speeches:
Mark my words, he shouted, on judgment day there will be weeping and gnashing of teeth.
I have no teeth, shouted one man. Undaunted the preacher shot back: teeth will be provided.

May God send you good fortune, contentment and peace, and may all your blessings forever increase.

Do you know why I was fired when I worked at the orange juice factory?
They said I couldn't concentrate.

When was tennis first mentioned in the bible?
When Joseph served in Pharaoh's court.

Did you hear about the Irish farmer who was awarded the Nobel Prize for being out standing in his field?

Did you hear about the Irish plumber looking at Niagara Falls?
He said: I think I can fix it.

What do you call a dog that can do magic tricks?
A Labracadabrador

A London taxi-man was approached, in the early hours of the morning, by a tall dark man with no arms who asked to be taken to the other side of town.
Taxi-man says: Ah, you look 'armless; 'op-in!

On the way back the same taxi man stopped to pick up three rather tipsy men who asked to be taken across town. The three tumbled into his taxi. On seeing how really drunk they were he had second thoughts, so he started up the engine, drove for one hundred yards and jammed on the breaks suddenly, and said: Ok guys we're here. Two of them jumped out but the third one complained. You should not drive so fast, You could kill someone.

I asked my librarian: Could you direct me to the self-help section, please?
No sir! she replied. If I told you that it would defeat the purpose.

Doctor: I have diagnosed your problem. It's onomatopoeia.
Patient: What's that?
Doctor: It's exactly what it sounds like.

He was bred in old Kentucky, but he's just a crumb up here.

A sign of an educated mind is that when it hears the William Tell overture it doesn't immediately think of The Lone Ranger. (Oldie but goodie.)

Big George had a dream in which he was eating this giant marshmallow and awoke to find that his pillow was gone.

The King's Knight was out on a wild stormy evening when his horse dropped dead. He stayed the night at a nearby Inn and after breakfast enquired if there was a horse in the stables he could buy, as he wished to continue on his Knightly duties for His Majesty the King. The Inn-keeper had no horses left in the stables but said: I do have something you could use, as he brought out this large Irish wolf-hound. The Knight took one look at the dog and said:You wouldn't send a Knight out on a dog like this?

As part of his act, a magician, on an ocean liner, was making one object after another, disappear. The ship's parrot, watching from the side, was not impressed by any of his tricks. It made him feel uncomfortable. Suddenly there was an explosion and the ship was blown to bits and pieces. The parrot found himself in the ocean on one end of a large piece of wood and the soaking wet magician on the other. The parrot studied the magician for a minute then said.
Ok! I give up. What did you do with the ship?

Barman to skeleton: What can I get you? Skeleton: A pint of beer and a mop, please. (I thought it was weak too but my son told it to me.)

The sexton told the parson, and the parson tolled the bell.

Husband: I think my wife must be an angel; she is always up in the air harping about something

The MO shouts out to new recruit: Carson!
Yes sir.
I did not see you at camouflage practice this morning?
Thank you sir.

I thought I'd finally met Mr. Right, but his first name was Always.

The new monk could only speak one sentence each year.

'First year he said: Cold floors.
Second year: Rotten food.
Third year: Hard bed.
Fourth year: I quit.
Head monk: Well, I'm not surprised that you're quitting; you've done nothing but complain since you got here.

Customer; Quick, line me up six Jack Daniels.
After watching the man drink them all in seconds, the barman says: Wow! I could never drink that much so fast.
Man: You would if you've got what I've got.
Barman: Oh, I'm sorry; is it cancer?
Man: No! It's a dollar.

......

I prefer to live in a world where all deeds done are greater than great deeds planned.

......

Driving home, after a late night drinking session, Murphy is pulled over by a policeman who gives him a telling off about his dangerous driving.
It might interest you, officer, Murphy explains, to know that I'm actually on my way to a lecture on the evils of drink and the dangers of drinking and driving.
Oh, really, said the cop and who's going to be giving a lecture like that at two in the morning?
Murphy: My wife.

Wife sends greeting card to her husband:
I'm so miserable here without you; it's almost like having you here.

The female 'handy-man' was given the job of painting red a gentleman's porch. She had given him a real low bid.
When she went outside the man's wife asked:
How can she possibly do our whole wrap-around porch for 100 dollars?
Sure enough she was finished in double quick time and after collecting her payment said to the man on the way out: Thanks for the work. By the way, it's a Jaguar you have not a Porsche.

Boy says to the preacher: When I grow up I am going to give you some money.
Well, thank you,. That's very nice of you said the preacher, but why?
Because my daddy says that you're the poorest preacher we've ever had here.

One drunk taking a short cut home across the dark cemetery fell in to a freshly dug grave. He tried in vain to climb out but gave up and, exhausted, he sat down in a corner and fell asleep. Sometime later a second drunk met the same fate and also fell in. Not aware of the other drunk sleeping he too tried repeatedly to climb out but kept falling back.

Waking up, the first drunk came up behind the second drunk and said: Give up you'll never make it. But he did.

No man ever had a scarf as warm as his daughter's arm around his neck.

Heard in bar: Do you remember that Gandhi fella. 'Quite a guy wasn't he? 'A bit of a one-day-wonder though. He just made that one movie, then we never heard of him again.

His first night in jail Maxie heard a prisoner shout out: Number 7 and all the other prisoners roared with laughter. Another prisoner shouted 33; more laughter. This reaction was repeated as other prisoners called out various numbers - much laughter at every new number. The next morning it was explained to him. Over time we have come to number all the jokes that we have told each other so that way we don't have to recite the joke, just the number.
That night Maxie decided to join in but when he called out a number there was only silence. What just happened he asked another inmate who told him: Ah! I guess, some people just don't know how to tell a joke?

Two really fanatical golfers stop their golf game as a funeral procession is passing by, in a nearby street. One takes off his cap, and asks his partner to join him in prayer for the deceased person. On resuming play his playing-partner asks: That was nice, but tell me, why did you do that?
He answered: Well, it was only right; you see we would have been married 44 years today.

John asks his dying friend Frank who, like himself is a great lover of baseball: Will you find a way to let me know if there is baseball in Heaven?
Sure enough, the following week Frank speaks to him from heaven: I have good news, John, and bad news. The good news is, there is indeed baseball in heaven and it's really wonderful.
John says: Oh, great but what's the bad news?

Frank: You're pitching on Tuesday.

Two fish swimming hit a wall, one says: Dam!

Molly was a lovely housewife living out in the 'boondocks'. She was a complete innocent in so many ways and certainly had never even seen an elephant until one day, there one was in their back garden, eating away at their potato patch. It had escaped from a traveling circus. In fright she ran back into the house calling to her husband:
Victor, come quick there's a monster in our potato patch.
What! What's it doing? He asked startled.
Molly: It's picking up the potatoes with its tail.

Yes, but what is it doing with them: asked Victor?
Molly hesitated, then said: If I told you, you wouldn't believe me.

From kids- for kids.

Teacher; why are you late?
Johnny: Class started before I arrived.

What's the best way to catch a unique, wild rabbit? Unique up on it.

What's the best way to catch a tame bunny? The tame way.

What's the best way to catch a squirrel?
Climb up a tree and act like a nut.

Where do ghosts best like to swim?
In the Dead Sea.

Acceptance of prevailing standards often means we have no standards.

Where is your humor bone? Your funny bone.

Why did the teddy bear not want to go to dinner? Because he was feeling stuffed.

What did the buffalo say to his son going off to college? Bi-son.

What makes walking on water easy? Freezing it.

Why was the skeleton too embarrassed to go to the Prom?
Because he had no body to go with.

Why did they call the elephant Dumbo?
That was his name. (Kids like it.)

Did you hear what happened the Sioux Indian who drank one hundred cups of tea in one evening?
The next morning they found him drowned in his own tepee.

Do you know how long cows should be milked?
Johnny: The same as short ones. (Right on. No difference' eh?)

Teacher: Donald, what is the chemical formula for water?
Donald: H I J K L M N O.
Teacher: What are you talking about?
Donald: Yesterday you said it's H to O

What did Tarzan say when he saw the elephant coming over the hill?
Here comes the elephant.

Teacher: Winnie, name one important thing we have today that we didn't have ten years ago
Winnie, smiling contentedly: Me! (Nice self esteem.)

Teacher: Millie, give me a sentence starting with ' I.'

Millie: I is.
Teacher: No, Millie, always say 'I am.'
Millie: Alright, 'I am the ninth letter of the alphabet.'

Teacher: George Washington not only chopped down his father's cherry tree, but also admitted it.
Now, Louis, do you know why his father didn't punish him?
Louis: Because George still had the axe in his hand?

What did Washington say to his men before they crossed the Delaware?
Get in the boat.

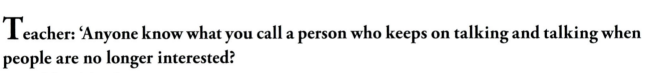

Teacher: Terence, your composition on 'My Dog' is exactly the same as your brother's. Did you copy his?
No sir said Terence; it's the same dog.

Teacher: 'Anyone know what you call a person who keeps on talking and talking when people are no longer interested?
Harold: A Teacher.

Teacher: John, why are you doing your math multiplication on the floor?
John: You told me to do it without using tables.

Little Jane to her friend: I sometimes wonder if God is pleased with me. Do you ever wonder, Mary, if God is pleased with you?
Mary, smiling contentedly, answers: He has to be. (thata girl)

How can you get four suits for a dollar?
Buy a deck of cards

How do you make an egg laugh?
Tell it a yolk.

What did the paper say to the pencil? Right on! (Write on)

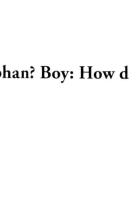

What bird can lift the most?
A crane.

Why did time go on strike?
I'll tell you in an hour.

Man to boy sitting all alone on the sidewalk: Are you an orphan? Boy: How did you know? What gave me away?
Man: Your parents, I guess.

What bone will a dog never eat?
A trombone.

Why do Eskimos always wash their clothes in Tide?
Because it's too cold out tide.

Teacher: Glenn, how do you spell crocodile?
Glenn answers: K-r-o-k-o-d-i-l-e
Teacher: No, that's wrong.
Glenn: It mighty be wrong, but you asked me how I spell it. (What a kid.)

Why do dragons sleep during the day?
So they can fight Knights.

What was the name of Noah's wife? Answer: Joan
Joan, how come?
Yes, Joan of Ark.

Some more for kids.

What can you hold without ever touching it?
A conversation.

What clothes does a house wear?
Address.

Why did the boy throw the clock out the window? Because he wanted to see time fly

What has six eyes but can't see?
Three blind mice.
What did the clown say when he jumped out of the closet? Surprise !!!!!! (I didn't think it was funny either)

What did baby corn say to mama corn? Where's popcorn? or Where's popcorn gone? (keep it going)

What kind of bears have no teeth?
Gummy bears.

What has one horn and gives milk without having to be milked?
A milk truck.

How do rabbits fix their hair? With a hare brush.

Why was the train late for its meeting? Because it was off-track.

A time when life was hard but simpler.

Mankind as a whole and Christians in particular are searching to find meaning purpose in a world that has become increasingly complicated and difficult to be happy in.

Why did the skunk cross the road? To get to the odor side.

Why did Cinderella yell at the soccer team? Because they kicked the ball.

What do you say when you meet a two-headed monster? Hello, hello! The man was wondering why the frisbee was getting closer and closer then it hit him.

Lady: I Didn't just marry an Irishman, I married him on St. Patricks day. Friend: Oh really! Lady: No, O'Reilly.

What Bible prophet was motherless?
Joshua, son of Nun.

Judge: Madame, is your appearance here this morning the result of a letter you got from the court? No judge; I usually dress this way.

Murphy was applying for a job on a building site:

Boss: Tell me, Mr Murphy, are you a sober man?
Murphy: Oh, yes indeed I am -- often.

What animal is most likely to eat a relative? An anteater

What flowers grow between your chin and your lip? Tulips.

Can February eat March? No, but April May.

One comedian to another: You surprised me tonight. You're usually so good.

The same Murphy was coming home after a long night of drinking. As he was about to use the escalator on the London Underground he saw a sign that read:
<u>Dogs must be carried on the escalator.</u>
He complained:
Oh where the heck am I going to find a dog at this time of night?

Patient: I worry all night long, I worry during the day. I worry all the time. What can I do? Psychiatrist says: Ah, I wouldn't worry about it. (Now that's a good one)

Psychiatrist: What's up?
Patient: Well, you see doctor I have this problem, I'm always telling lies.
Psychiatrist: I don't believe you.
His next patient says: My problem is that I'm always losing my temper over silly things.
Pardon? says the psychiatrist.
Patient: What the heck! I've already told you once.

Doctor to the Old Hill-Billy: How well do you sleep?
Hill-Billy: I sleep very well at night, tolerably well in the morning but in the afternoon I get a bit restless.

It is customary on building sites for the new guy to make the tea in a large kettle for all the crew. Murphy was being interviewed for a job. Boss asks:
Mr. Murphy, can you make tea?
Murphy: Oh yes, certainly I can. Boss: Can you drive a fork-lift?
Murphy: Why? How big is the kettle?

The Postman is about to open the gate as the lady is standing by her door waiting for the mail. He closes the gate quickly when he sees a fierce looking dog standing by her side.
He asks: Madame does your dog bite?
No, she says: He walks up to her and hands her the mail. The dog bites him on the leg.
'Real put-out he shouts: Madame, I thought you said your dog doesn't bite. Lady: That's not my dog.

A policeman in a crowded room, picks up a hat from the floor and, holding it in the air, calls out to a man leaving the room: Sir, is this your hat?
No thanks, says the man, I'm not that tall.
Ok, it's daft.

I had a joke about unemployment but it's not working.

I had this joke about mountain climbing but I haven't made it up yet.

Our grandparent's Kilcoo cottage in Co. Down N. Ireland.
(Twelve happy children born under that little red roof.)

Man falls off the Effill Tower-fifty feet and goes splat on the ground. People run over shouting: What happened? What happened? The man looking up says: I don't know; I just got here myself.
Man: Isn't prejudice a terrible thing, Fred?
Fred: Well, thank God no one can say that about me. I'm not prejudiced, I hate everyone.

Jack: I was so worried but you were right John I didn't get fired I was promoted.
John: Well you see Jack I have faced a hundred crises in my life and most of them never happened

If one needs some comfort Dial a Prayer service will supply you with some words from Holy Scripture.
The atheists, as a group, demanded 'equal time' so the telephone company obliged them by giving them their own number.
Now, you just dial their number and nobody answers.

<u>Life is one long lesson in humility.</u>

If at first you don't succeed, give up.

If at first you don't succeed bury the evidence that you tried.

You know the patient's getting better if he takes a turn for the nurse.

What did the zero say to the eight? Nice belt. (I didn't get it either, at first)

My friend thinks he's a chicken.
Well tell him he's not.
I can't do that.
Why not?
I need the eggs.

My wife said she wanted diamonds so I bought her a deck of cards.

Two fanatical golfer's, one says: Buddy: How are things?
His partner responds: Not so good. Since last we met I've lost both my wife <u>and</u> my putter and I really miss it.

Hard-drinking Pat at bar: There are two drinks I want to try before I die, water and a cup of tea.

Guy in the Pharmacy: Could you give me something for loss of voice?
The girl says: Can I help you sir?

Driving home, after a late night drinking session, Murphy is pulled over by a policeman who gives him a telling off about his dangerous driving.
It might interest you, officer, Murphy explains, to know that I'm actually on my way to a lecture on the evils of drink and the dangers of drinking and driving.
Oh, really, said the cop. And who's going to be giving a lecture like that at two in the morning? Murphy: My wife.

Wife to her husband: Harry, honey, we have to stop all this quarreling; I know I'm a very difficult person to get along with, but don't worry, you'll change.

Did you hear about the two frogs that had parked illegally? They were toad away.

Customs officer: Sir, are you carrying any pornography with you.
No, said Paddy, I don't even have a phonogram.

What happens when two Greeks meet? They greet each other.

It's the way I tell Them

Two jumper cables go into a bar and the barman says: Look! I don't mind serving you two guys, as long as you promise not to start something.

Did you hear about the man who was very pleased with himself because he completed the jigsaw puzzle in 30 minutes, even though it said on the box 5-6 years?

Old Irish mother to her neighbor:
I was thinking the other night how I'm so lucky. I started out in life with nothing and I still have most of it with me. (Yogi Berra had nothing on us Irish.)

Judge: Mr. Bates, you have been found innocent of these burglary and robbery charges. You can leave this court now, your reputation unstained.
Mr. Bates: Thank you, judge. Does that mean I can keep the jewels?

A man's truck broke down miles from home. A kind passer by offered to tow it so the man went searching for help at a nearby farmhouse. He needed a strong rope to help tow the truck back for repairs. As he approached the house he noticed an old, long, but strong looking rope that seemed to have been tossed aside in a field for years, it had mud and grass covering parts of it. When he explained his predicament and asked the farmer could he borrow the rope the farmer said he could not. The man pleaded with him promising that he would bring it back. I'm using it said the farmer. Why it's been lying there for years explained the man, please let me borrow it. No! said the farmer, I'm using it.
You're using it; what are you using it for that I can't borrow it for a short time? I use it to help milk the goats with replied the farmer. How could a rope like that be of any possible use in milking a goat, the man asked. Look mister! said the farmer, when you don't want to do something one excuse is as good as another. (I know when I'm beaten.)

An old man goes to answer a knock on his door one evening to find two somber looking sheriff deputies standing there.
Sir, are you married? One deputy asked.
Why yes, the old man replied, for 48 years.
Do you have a photograph of your wife by any chance? Said the second deputy.
The old man pulled a picture out of his wallet and handed it to the officers. They looked it over and handed it back to him.
Then one said to him: Sir, I'm sorry to have to tell you but it appears that your wife has been hit by a truck.
The old man says, Yes sir, but she's got a lovely personality and she's a great cook.
(Ah, It's kind of sweet.)

A man sits down to dinner with his wife. There is a loud knock on the door. The man calls out, who is it? It's the Boston Strangler. The man answers: Honey it's for you
(Alright, it's NOT funny?)

A father was at his wits awful at a public school then no better at a private school. Reports on his conduct were worse. Even when he sent him to a tough army school there was little improvement. In desperation his father enrolled him in a catholic school. At the end of his very first term he came home with a report card showing both good conduct and A's in every subject.
Amazed his father asked why the sudden change.
His son explained: Well! You see dad, when I saw that guy up there on the cross I knew that they meant business.

Pope John XXIII (now canonized a saint) was also known for his wit.
A reporter was interviewing him while walking in the Vatican grounds where all kinds of tradesmen were working.
Curious the reporter asked: About how many people do you think are working here at the Vatican?
The Pope replied: About half of them I'd say.

His election as Pope- John XXIII, was a big surprise to all as he was getting on in years. Too old to be Pope some thought. Some say the Cardinals could not agree on any one of the three front-runners so they choose him as an interim Pope - a nice jolly sort of fellow who wouldn't be there too long anyway. So there was great laughter when he addressed the Conclave Cardinals for the first time after his election, saying:
Well! Here I am at the end of the road and top of the heap.

The best way to make holy water is to boil the hell out of it.

My grandfather has not been feeling well. He said:
I knew I wasn't well last week when I was walking past the cemetery and two guys ran after me with shovels.

Headline in Ireland's Cork Examiner newspaper: Man found dead in graveyard.

Murphy had been out drinking and his car was swerving all over the road. A cop stopped him- stuck his head in the window and said: You're drunk!
Murphy: Oh thanks be to God officer; for a minute I thought my steering had gone!

A little boy was attending his first wedding. After the service, his aunt asked him: How many times do you think a man can marry? Sixteen, the boy responded. Really? How did you come up with that number? Easy, the little boy said. All you have to do is add it up, like the pastor said:
4 better, 4 worse, 4 rich and 4 poorer. sixteen."

Do you know why you should never marry a tennis player?
You never marry a tennis player because to a tennis player LOVE means nothing.

A boy was watching his father, a pastor, write a sermon,
How do you know what to say? He asked.
Why, God tells me.
Oh, then why do you keep crossing things out?

A little girl became restless as the preacher's sermon dragged on and on. Finally, she leaned over to her mother and whispered, Mommy, if we give him the money now, will he let us go?

Murphy says to his friend: I've decided to build a pigsty at the end of my house for the pigs.
But what about the smell? His friend asks.
Murphy: Sure the pigs don't mind.

Little Patrick was determined to have Santa bring him a bicycle for Christmas. Early in December he wrote a letter to God asking Him to put a word in for him with Santa. I really, really want a bike, he wrote.
As Christmas drew near and there was no response he grew desperate.
Up he went to his room and took down a statue of Mary the Mother of God. He wrapped

it in two towels and hid it away as best he could so no one would find it. Then he sat down and wrote another note to God, which read:
Dear God if you ever want to see your mother again you better get me that bike. (I bet that did the trick)

They said that the life-guard refused to save the hippie because he was too far out.

The harp that once through Tara's walls. You'll hear her play no more. The Saxon's came- they of ill fame. And drove us from our shore.

One of my sons, troubadour
'Obo' Martin Mc Crory.

Troubadour 'Obo' Martin - Mc Crory.

I find myself here tonight to honor this second rate comedian. That shows you where my career's heading.

Even a blind hog finds some acorns.

An American tourist goes up to a farmer milking his cow on the brow of a hill.
He asks: Could you give me directions to the nearest village?
The farmer obliges, and the man thanks him.
The tourist then asks: Could you also tell me what time it is?
To his surprise, the farmer lifted up the cow's udders in his hands, and says: It is ten minutes to two.
Why, that's amazing! Said the tourist. Do you mean to tell me you can tell the time by the weight of the cow's udders?
Don't be silly. Said the farmer. You see, when I lift the udders high enough, I can see the village clock.

A hypocrite is someone who writes a book on atheism and prays that it sells

He who eats too many prunes gets a good run for his money

The camping-equipment store was having a giant winter sale. The sign in the window read: This is the winter of our discount tents.
(Think Shakespeare if that doesn't seem funny.)

Comedian: Hey, what's all this about these people who say:
Oh, I remember where I was when Elvis died?
Heck, I remember where I was nearly all the time.

I lost my job recently. Well, I didn't actually lose it. I know where it is; it's just that when I go there, someone else is doing it

A sick old codger says:
It isn't the cough that'll carry me off, it's the coffin they'll carry me off in.

Question: Can an atheist get insurance against an act of God???

Just think, if it were not for venetian blinds it would be curtains for all of us.

Doctor to patient: Do you want the good news or the bad news first?
The patient asks for the good news.
The doctor says: Sorry but you've only got 24 hours left to live
Patient says: Whao! Well then, what's the bad news"?
Doctors says: I should have told you yesterday.
(Some doctor!)

Did your date with the Siamese twins go well?
Yes and no

Pattie Finn's wife died when she received a kick in the head from her donkey.
At her funeral, all the locals were taken aback by how many men from all over the county followed the funeral procession.
One local stopped one of the men and said: I didn't know Maggie had so many male friends?
The stranger replied: Oh, we're not friends. We're all here hoping to buy the donkey

Man says: I'd like a pound of sausages, please.
Butcher answers: We only sell kilo's here.
Man says: Ok, I'll have a pound of kilos

The truth does not decompose; no matter how long you cover it up it's still always there.

Two spiders crawling up a wall. One says:

You should really check out my new web site.

What do you call a camel with three humps? Humphrey.

Nothing like a good Laugh...

A man fell off a cliff but managed to save himself by grabbing onto a small tree branch. Hanging on for dear life he yelled out for help. Is there anybody up there? Help me please. Help! Help! Then heard a voice: This is God speaking. Oh, yes God help me please; I can't hold on much longer. Do you believe in me, God asks. Yes I do, I do. Help me; I don't want to die.

Do you trust me? God continues. I do. I do.
Do you really trust me? Yes God, the man assures Him.
Then LET GO, says God.
There is SILENCE. After a few minutes the man shouts up the cliff: Is there anybody else up there?

A little nun at a bus stop goes into a faint. A man behind catches her and moves her over to a bench outside a bar. I'll get you something to drink, he says. What would you like?
Nun: Oh, could I have a whiskey and water please.
Sure, he says as he leaves.
She calls out to him. And could you please ask them to put it in a paper cup.
Inside the barman says: What can I get you sir?
A whiskey and water please.
Certainly, said the barman.
And could you please put it in a paper cup, the man adds.
Oh my, says the barman, is that wee nun here again?

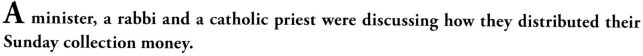

A minister, a rabbi and a catholic priest were discussing how they distributed their Sunday collection money.
The minister says: I just draw a circle like this - throw all the money up in the air and what lands in the circle is mine and the rest is God's.

The rabbi says. I draw a somewhat smaller circle, throw up the money and whatever lands outside the circle is mine, the rest is God's.

The priest says: I have no need of a circle; I just throw it ALL up to God; whatever he wants he takes. The rest is mine. That works fine for me.

Irish wit:
The bachelor farmer was tired of being single so he put an advertisement in the classifieds, just two words"
Wife wanted.
Almost immediately he got one hundred replies; they all said the same thing:
You can have mine.

A man flattened by his opponent can get up again and fight on, but a man flattened by conformity will stay down.

The first man Adam was lonely so God came to his aid. I will give you a great companion; you'll love her. She is so beautiful and smart and will do everything you ask and never cause you any trouble- not for one minute but in return you must give me one arm or a leg. Ah! No God, I don't want that, says Adam. He thought for a minute then asked: Lord, what would you give me for just one rib?

How's business? His friend asked.
Well, as you know, I was not just breeding turkeys, I was breeding four-legged turkeys.
How is it going?
It went bust.
How come?
I couldn't catch them. (Imagine the chase.)

A man wearing a mask robs a bank. As he turns to leave a man is looking straight at him.
Did you just see me rob the bank? he asked him.
Yes, said the man.
The robber shoots him.

He turns to a man standing with his wife and asks: Did you see me rob the bank? No, I did not, he answered, but my wife did.

I would no sooner write free verse than play tennis with the net down. And then I bought a book on free verse; it cost me $12

Fiction is good when its goal is to reveal truth but evil if perverted and evil when its purpose is to spread lies.

My friend was consoling me, saying: Cheer up, things could be worse. So I took his advice. He was right too. I cheered up and things got worse.

When I was young, my family was so poor they used to buy all my clothes at the Goodwill store.
I used to look ridiculous going to school dressed like a Japanese admiral.

So, a Doctor is perturbed at a party because a lot of his friends are telling him their symptoms and asking for his free medical advice. He sees an attorney friend and asks him what he does when people come up to him at parties asking for legal advice. He tells him he gives advice and send them a bill and then they don't bother him again. A fe thew days later doctor was wondering if that tactic would work for him when a letter arrived with a bill from the lawyer for his advice at the party.

I grilled a chicken for twenty minutes yesterday and it still refused to tell me why it crossed the road.

County Down N. Ireland: They call it the basket of eggs with it's beautiful rolling hills.

....
Some more jokes for the road:
Husband: I married for better or for worse; my wife couldn't do better and I couldn't do worse. (But you know that's not true!)

True love is free. It is not practiced to achieve other ends.

Never get so busy making a living that you forget to make a life.

I've been married a long time and it hasn't been half-bad. You see I'm away half the time.

Murphy stumbles into the confessional box ahead of a long line of waiting penitents and the priest says : Paddy are you drunk? No, says Paddy, I just want you to hear my confession. Are you sure you're not drunk Paddy? No I'm fine, I'm just here for confession. Father says. Tell me Paddy did you commit murder. Paddy says. No father. Priest says. Ok Paddy come back next week and I'll hear your confession. Paddy staggers out of the confession box and tells everyone. Best you all go home now;father's only hearing murder cases this week.

I think that anyone who believes in capital punishment ought to be hanged.

The Postman is about to open the gate as the lady is standing by her door waiting for the mail. He closes the gate quickly when he sees a fierce looking dog standing by her side.
He asks: Madame does your dog bite?
No, she says: He walks up to her and hands her the mail. The dog bites him on the leg. 'Real put-out he shouts: Madame, I thought you said your dog doesn't bite. Lady: That's not my dog.

I have not spoken to my wife for three weeks; I didn't want to interrupt her. A bachelor is a man who has not made the same mistake once.

Why did the cat visit the hospital? To get a cat scan.

The way to become an alcoholic is to have a drink and then you feel like a new man and then you need a drink to celebrate. (Not funny?)

Rich or poor it's always nice to have money.

The half-undressed patient is being examined by the quack doctor who says:
The first thing you've got to do is cut out all health foods for a while. That will be $200. The nurse will return your clothes with the receipt.

English humor:
What did the gas meter say to the shilling? I'm glad you popped in Bob. I was just going out.

Fred Blogs, holding up his cup of tea, says to his friend Alfie Bates: Alfie, there's nothing like a good cup of tea - and this is nothing like a good cup of tea.

Say what you mean; mean what you say but don't say it mean.
On being honored with the keys of the city Bob Hope quipped: I feel very humbled by this but I think I have the strength of character to fight it.

A Mr. John Mc Kinney died leaving his wife a widow. At the same time, another unrelated Mr. John McKinney took off on a business trip to Arizona. He sent his wife a card, which was mistakenly mailed to the late Mr. McKinney's. The card read: I just arrived. A second card followed. It's really hot here.

A huge hole was discovered in Trafalgar Square, London.

'First reports say that the police are looking into it.

Money should be at the service of man not man the slave of money.

Trainer: I have a horse that walks normally sometimes and sometimes it limps. What can I do? Veterinarian: The next time it walks normally sell it.

A sign of wealth is when a bald man gets a haircut.

You know what the stork does. Well this stork is flying around and he has an old man in his pouch/sack. The man is saying to the stork: Will you at least admit we're lost?

If swimming is good for the figure how do you explain a whale?

Son: Daddy what is arbitration? Father: A skill learned when living with three teenagers and one car.

I know this guy who has an addiction to soap but he insists he's clean.
Doctor to elderly patient: Well, I'm afraid I have to tell you that you have cancer AND you have alzheimer's Patient says: Ah well, at least I don't have cancer.

Dan was a single guy living at home with his father, who is a widower, and worked in the family business. When he found out he was going to inherit a fortune when his sickly father died, he decided he needed to find a wife with whom to share his fortune.

One evening, at an investment meeting, he spotted the most beautiful woman he had ever seen. Her natural beauty took his breath away.
"I may look like just an ordinary guy," he said to her, "but in just a few months, my sickly father will die and I will inherit $200 million."
Impressed, the woman asked for his business card.

Three days later, she became his step-mother.

What did one candle say to the other candle? Are you going out tonight?

The early bird catches the worm but the second mouse gets the cheese.

The reason lobsters NEVER share is because they are shellfish.

Murphy has only been in prison eight months but in that short time he has managed to have his tonsils taken out his appendices taken out and all his teeth removed. He is back in for another operation. The warden now suspects that he may be trying to escape bit by bit.

Passing a spiked-haired elderly lady a guy comments: She looks like she was pardoned after the warden threw the switch. (Think Phyllis Diller)

I was going to tell you this unemployment joke but it's not working.

I had a mountain climbing joke as well but I haven't made it up yet.
(Two repeats for you to learn.)

If you had five pinions (small nuts) in one hand and four pinions in the other hand what would you have? You'd have a difference of a pinion.

When the Scotsman won millions on the lottery and was asked by a reporter what he would do now about begging letters, he replied:
Oh, I will still send them.

You always know the patient is getting better when he takes a turn for the nurse.

Two innocent children, a boy and a girl are talking:
The little boy says: I'm a boy and you're a girl.
How do you know that, she says.
He pulls up his long T-shirt and points down saying,
Look, BLUE boots.

I asked my wife why she threw out the vacuum cleaner. She said: I had to, it was just gathering dust.

I was thinking that if this joke book doesn't sell well I'm going to try to open a joint account with someone who has money. (A good idea or not?)

At the racetrack, last week, a man was shot with a starter's pistol. The police think it might be race related.

Say what you like about deaf people. (It's a good one.)

Why was the doughnut unhappy? He was feeling crummy.

Front page headline in the Cork Examiner:
Man kills self then wife and child.
A man mistakenly drank a pint of varnish. It was a horrible death but a beautiful finish.

Boss, interviewing Murphy for building site job, says: Do you ever drink to excess?

Murphy: Oh yes indeed, I'll drink to anything. Boss: No, I mean are you a sober man? Murphy replies: Oh yes I am, often.

A man fell off the Eiffel Tower, nine hundred feet and landed splat on the ground. People ran over saying : What happened,? What happened? Looking up he said: I don't know, I just got here myself.

If you don't read the newspapers you are uninformed. If you do read the newspapers you are misinformed.

Diamonds are forever because that's how long it takes to pay for them.
When Henry Ford visited Ireland some years ago a large hospital was being built in the town where his ancestors came from. The Fund Raising group lost no time in approaching him to make a donation towards a new wing they had decided upon. In honor of your folks. they said. We will even put your name on it with a nice appropriate scriptural quote above it. He agreed to donate 50,000 American dollars. The next day the committee had a front page story with the headline Henry Ford donates 500,000 to new hospital. He protested to them: I only promised 50,000 not 500,000. No problem they said, tomorrow morning we'll print a front page retraction explaining our mistake and that it was only 50,000. Ford responded. Oh, I see where you are going with this. Look I WILL make it 500,000 on condition that I get to choose my own scriptural quote for the building. Done deal, they said.
So if you go there today, at the hospital entrance, under the name Henry Ford is his scripture quotation I CAME AMONGST YOU
AND YOU TOOK ME IN.

Kilcoo, Co. Down, N. Ireland.

There was a time when this road was packed with young and old men and women going to church on Sunday but, sadly, " The land of saints and scholars " is no more.

….. …..The three wives tale: (and one tough Irish women)

The first man married a woman from Italy. He told her that she was to do the dishes and house cleaning. It took a couple of days, but on the third day, he came home to see a clean house and dishes washed and put away.
The second man married a woman from Poland. He gave his wife orders that she was to do all the cleaning, dishes and the cooking. The first day he didn't see any results, but the next day he saw it was better. By the third day, he saw his house was clean, the dishes were done and there was a huge dinner on the table. The third man married a girl from Ireland. He ordered her to keep the house clean, dishes washed, lawn mowed, laundry washed, and hot meals on the table for every meal. He said the first day he didn't see anything, the second day he didn't see anything but by the third day, some of the swelling had gone and he could see a little out of his left eye, and his arm was healed enough that he could fix himself a sandwich and load the dishwasher. He still has some difficulty when he pees……….

One math book to another math book: How's it going? Response: Well, we sure got a lot of problems.

There was a young man from Dageeling on the bus from London to Ealing. The sign on the door said don't spit on the floor so he carefully spat on the ceiling.

Church custodian- as he picks up a paper bag from under the pew. Father, you may want to cut down on the length of your sermons. They are starting to bring their lunches with them.

Patient: One day doctor I feel like a wigwam and other days I feel like a tepee. What is that?
Psychiatrist: That's an easy one, you're just two tents. (tense)
I take my wife everywhere but she always manages to find her way back.
After an hour long sermon the pastor finally stops and asks the congregation: Is there anything else you'd like me to add. One man shouts back: How about an Amen.

……..

A ship is safe in harbor but that is not what a ship is made for. If you harbor bitterness happiness will dock at some other port. …….
My neighbor is more than a friend to me. He's a total stranger.

A football team had a poor record last year 4 wins and and 20 losses. Well, what do you expect from a team called the Blackbirds?

My friend thinks he's a great comedian.
"I have a great delivery." He says.
(Yeah, it belongs on a dump truck.)

Married lady says; Things have been hard for me financially since my husband died.
Her friend says: Really ! I thought you said that your husband left you twenty-five thousand dollars?
Yes but I used five thousand on the funeral expenses and the other twenty thousand on a memorial stone.
Her friend asks: Oh, that must have been a BIG stone?
Married lady: Yes, two and a half carat.

When is a door not a door? When it's ajar.
Following on the heels of his fellow comedian as he walked off the stage, he turns to him

and says, Bernie, I'd really like to say how funny you were tonight. I can't. (The truth is he just doesn't like that guy.)
((Not the greatest MC.))
Good ladies evening and gentlemen, our next speaker needs no introduction, he hasn't showed up. In retrospect, or hindsight and looking back, we ought not to have invited him. (The same for yourself.)

Coming down from the mountain with the three tablets, containing the Fifteen Commandments, Moses says: God has sent me to bring you these Fifteen… (one tablet falls and breaks)… these Ten Commandments.

That might explain why we know that God will never send another flood on the world. How? Well, the first one was useless. Ok!

Everyone but atheists have a holiday. Actually they do have a holiday. It's called April Fools Day.

One strawberry says to other strawberry? If you weren't so fresh we wouldn't be in this jam.

Sign in music shop: Gone Chopin - Bach in a minute.

Blind date blues: To his bored-stiff date, Arnold, says: Enough talk about me. Let's talk about all the stuff I own. (Oh, my!)

On an overnight train journey a mother places her youngest child up in the overhead bunk saying: You'll be alright. God will watch over you. God is with you. Some minutes later the chid asks Mother are you there? Yes, I am here she answers. Minutes later: Father are you there? Yes, I am here he says. Then again: Mother are you there? Yes son. This question and answering went on for awhile until one of the other passengers, anxious for some sleep answered: Yes! Your mother is here. Your father is here. Your brothers and sisters are here. Everybody's here. We are all here!
Silence ensued for several minutes, then the little boy in a hushed voice said: Mother, Was that God?

A pun, a limerick and a play–on-words walk into a bar. No joke!

John's wife ran away with his best friend George. George wasn't his best friend until he ran away with his wife.

That sounds like the same guy who said: I've been married for forty years and it seems like just five minutes — under water. (Bad!!!!!)

Wife: You lied to me before you married me. You said you were well off. Husband: I was but I didn't know it.
Comedian: And now I will introduce to you Mr. Joe Wilson: Joe and I have been friends for a long time. There are many reasons for that but mostly bad luck.

The young man was asked by his prospective father in-law: Son, can you afford to support a family? Young man says: Well, no sir. I was just planning to support your daughter, the rest of you will have to fend for yourselves. (No flies on him. Worth repeating.)

The reason there are no telephone directory's in China is because there are so many Wings and Wongs there that they are afraid someone will wing a wong number.
Charles: How are your counseling sessions going? Robert: Well, I still have that fear of elevators but I'm taking steps to correct it.
You know you got a drinking problem, in the early hours of the morning, when you get a ticket for zig-zagging on the freeway- -- -- -- without a car.
The devil appeared in church one day and everyone scattered every which way; even the priest ran away. One man stayed, sitting there staring at the devil. The devil leaned forward and said: Well why are you not running away? He replied: Well, as you know, I live with your sister.

What clothing did a mermaid wear to her math class? An algebra.
Where do mermaids go to watch movies ? The dive-in.
Anger management class the instructor asks: Are things any better for you now? Student answers, it's hard to say. If it were not for people I'd be able to get along with everyone.
What did the beach say to the ocean? Nice to sea ya ! What did the ocean say to the beach? Nothing, he just waved.
Teacher: Does anyone know the Garden of Eden story ? Willie, the class wit, (or nitwit) answered. Well I Know that Adam blamed Eve and that Eve blamed the devil and that the devil didn't have a leg to stand on. (Guys like him made tough school days more bearable for me.)

An aspiring author submitted his manuscript for assessment to a large publishing company. They replied: Your manuscript was both good and original. The part that was good was not original and the part that was original was not good.

(But I believe even Mark Twain got rejections like that.) Undaunted the same author takes his manuscript in person to another publishing company. He is met at the gate by the security guard: Can I help you sir? the guard says. Yes, I'd like to give my manuscript to the publisher, in person. Guard: He is not here today, sir, but if you give it to me I can reject it for you.
(That's just about right.)

A man runs into the doctors office and says: Doctor there's an invisible man outside who says he wants to talk to you. What should I tell him? Doctor says: Tell him I can't see him today. (Worth reprinting)

The little ant grew up confused; he could not understand how all his uncles were 'aunts'. Just think: If every car in America was pink in color we'd have a pink car nation.

Plump gentleman standing at hospital reception desk with a giant arrow stuck all the way through his body from stomach and way out his back. Sorry, the nurse says, 'Doctors out until Tuesday; can you not sleep on your side.

First man to another at entrance to the psychiatrist office: Are you coming or going? Second man: If I knew that I wouldn't be here.

Say what you like about deaf people.
On the other hand, you have different fingers.

The warden to convict in electric chair: Is there one last
thing I can do for you? Prisoner: Yes, hold my hand.
Did you hear about the hump-backed convict who was bent on going straight?

Custom Inspector at the airport to young woman: Have you been abroad? No sir, she says, I've always been a lady. (I'm sure he had a good laugh at that)
First the husband dies and goes to heaven. His wife dies soon after and also goes to heaven. On seeing her husband she exclaims; Oh honey, after fifty years of marriage we are together again. He says: Oh no, that was just until death do us part. (so sad)

Shawn says: Johnny tells us you are planning something big. Erica : Forget Johnny. Sure half the lies he tells aren't true.

Do you know why eskimos are so religious? It's because they are God's frozen people.

Do you know what song Eskimo's sing at birthdays?
You've heard it before: Freeze a jolly good fellow

Blubber is the fat of a whale:
Guy sticks his head in the igloo and says: Any blubber here?
Eskimo replies: No blubbers – two sisters.

Do you know how an Eskimo builds his house?
Igloos it all together.

Too many prominent people consider themselves anointed messengers for the rest of us They equate their success with verification that they must lead the way for the rest of us mere mortals.

As a city boy I spent all my, unforgettable, childhood summers here in the roads and fields where the great Saint Patrick tended his sheep.

In Russia things are not as plentiful as they are here. There are long lines for food, even shortage of necessities at times.

Lady in store asks: Have you any meat or are you all out of meat? Owner: Oh, no it is the store across the street that's all out of meat. We are the store that is all out of milk.

Do you know why you never see a blind man sky dive? Because it's hard on the dog. It's a good one.

Cocky entertainer : Did you like my show? Response : You were great if you're any kind of a judge.

Knock knock: Who's there? Too. Too who? No, to whom?

Because I could not stop for death he kindly stopped for me. The carriage held but just ourselves and immortality.

Conversation in court:

Q: Doctor, before you performed the autopsy, did you check for a pulse? A.: No.

Q: Did you check for blood pressure? A; No.
Q: Did you check for breathing? A: No.
Q: So, it is possible the patient was alive when you began the autopsy? A: No. Q: How can you be so sure? A: Because his brain was sitting on my desk in a jar.
Q: But could the patient have still been alive, nevertheless?
A: Yes, it is possible that he could have been alive and practicing law somewhere.

I've clerked in Kansas city, sold insurance in Saint Paul Peddled books in Dallas Texas and gone hungry in them all.

Religion teacher: Does anyone know what a dogma is? Johnny says. Is it a mother of pups?

Do you know why you will never see a twelve inch nose on a person or even an animal? Because then it would not be a nose but a foot.

Romeo and Juliet, in a restaurant they met. Short of cash to pay the debt, Romeo owed what juliet. Insert image no.128

Denial is not just a river in Egypt.
If you jumped off the Paris bridge you'd be in-Seine.

If a bricklayer can lay bricks why can't a plumber…..

It rained all night the day I left. The weather it was dry. The sun so hot I froze to death. Susanna don't you…

(Cry, not die is the right answer.)

Two antennas got married. It was a lousy wedding but a great reception.

I used to think I was indecisive but now I'm not so sure.

Why should you always keep up your payments to your exorcist? Because you don't want to be repossessed

There was a young man from Ingels - operated on for the shingles. They sewed up his hide, left the scissors inside so now when he dances he jingles.

I was at the theater watching a sad movie the other night. The lady behind me was wailing; the next thing I knew I felt this harpoon in my back.

….to a little cabin built there of clay and wattles made. (Who wrote that?)

There was a young man from Athlone who ate onions and leeks by the stone When he went to the dance he hadn't a chance for the girls left him strictly alone. The sales executive, lying on the psychiatric couch, says: Can I have the marketing rights to your ceiling?

The warden says to the prisoner on the electric chair; Is there one last thing I can do for you, the warden asks the prisoner on the electric chair. Yes, said the prisoner; hold my hand. (Remember it)

There was a young man from Dageeling on a bus from London to Ealing. The sign on the door said DON'T SPIT ON THE FLOOR so he kindly spat on the ceiling.

I read about this poor peanut walking down the street and was assaulted.

Speaking of their friend after his funeral one woman said: He was a saint, he was. Yes, he was, the other lady fervently agreed, but even more than that he was a nice man. I would think so. There was a young schoolboy named billy Who's answers were sometimes quite silly One day he was told Name a country that"s cold And poor silly Billy said Chile.

In religion class teacher asks. Anyone know what Buddha is? Johnny says. Its what I spread on my toast.

Teacher: What's another name for God?says Shelia:Harold? Teacher: Harold? Yes, you know, Our father who art in heaven, Harold be thy name. I'm reading this great book on Gravity. I can't put it down. What would you be if you jumped off the Paris bridge? You'd be in Seine.

Why should one never make fun of fat people? No, because they already have enough on their plate.

This is a precious photo of my mother's family in Co Down Northern Ireland, My grandfather and grandmother - holding some of the children. My mother Maggie was one of twelve children- five girls and seven boys. I am one of four boys and four girls. My wife is one of two girls and six boys. ("Blessed is the man who has filled his quiver with them; he shall not be put to shame when he contends with his enemy at the gate.")

Teacher: What's another name for God?
Shelia says :Harold?
Teacher: Harold? Yes, you know, Our father who art in heaven, Harold be thy name.
I'm reading this great book on Gravity. I can't put it down.
What would you be if you jumped off the Paris bridge? You'd be in Seine.
Why should one never make fun of fat people? No, because they already have enough on their plate.

Sign in church bulletin. Tonight the service topic is " What is hell?" Come early and listen to our choir practice.
A great start to professor's Philosophy class; he says:
If wisdom's ways you wisely seek, five things observe with care, of whom you speak, to whom you speak and why and when and where.
What was the name of Noah's wife? It was Joan. Joan? Yes, Joan of Ark.
Why should you never iron a four leaf clover? Because you don't want to press your luck.

What is another way of describing two thieves? A pair of nickers. (to nick- to steal something - English slang.)

Why do witches always wear name tags? Witches wear name tags so that each witch will know which witch is which. (A good one)

Psychiatrist: Does your family suffer from mental illness? Lady: No, I don't think so. I think they rather enjoy it.

Rodney Dangerfield was complaining on the Johnny Carson Show. Oh my wife hates me and my son is evil ; he doesn't like me at all. I get no respect. I got no luck at all. At the first race at the track last week, when the starters pistol went off it shot my horse. (May he rest in peace - Rodney, I mean, not the horse.)

………,

A weary hitch-hiker thought he'd never catch a ride as darkness approached when, to his delight, a car stopped to pick him up. Climbing in he showed his appreciation. You know it is really nice of you to stop for me I mean it's late at night and you don't know me. I could be a serial killer or anything. The driver replied. I have no fear of that for what are the chances of having two serial killers in a car at the same time? (Oh my!)

I am sure that wherever my father is now he's looking down on us. He's not dead, he's just very condescending.

I was watching the two men racing to get the first place prize. One was dressed like a chicken, the other was dressed like an egg. I thought to myself: This could be be interesting.

The Narcoleptic Society called a three to four pm emergency meeting but no one showed up; they were asleep.

Money will not, buy you happiness but it can buy you the kind of misery you prefer and it can make you more comfortable while you are being miserable. (Can't argue with that.)

Where would you find a tortoise with no arms and no legs? Where you left him. (Not nice at all.)

It's Valentines Day as I end this book.
A soldier was sitting alone in a restaurant when he was approached by a concerned patriotic American.
I'm sorry sir to see you sitting all alone on Saint Valentine's day. Hold it there buddy, says the soldier; I didn't lose a leg in Vietnam just to sit alone on Valentine's Day. Lose a leg? the man protested, but, sir, you have both your legs. Soldier: That's what I said, I didn't lose a leg in Vietnam.

My doctor said I was hard of hearing.
I haven't heard from him since.

Parting thought!
When I was young people used to laugh at me when I said I wanted to be a comedian.
Well, nobody's laughing now. (Scratch that. -:)

                                                       The End.

I want you all to know
I've had a wonderful time.

But this wasn't it. -:)

Just joking.

To have a sense of humor Lord
The grace to see a joke
To see the funny things in life
'Pass on to other folk.

One half in heaven, one half on earth Of earthly toil and heavenly mirth A wonderful woven scene.

G. K. Chesterton tells us:

Laughter has something in common with the ancient winds of faith and inspiration; it unfreezes pride and unwinds secrecy; it makes men forget themselves in the face of something greater than themselves. It can even be used at times of great suffering.

In 1974, my wife Marie and I (married fifty years now) arrived in San Francisco from trouble-torn Belfast, Northern Ireland. I had received a scholarship to play soccer for the University of San Francisco. It was our passage out of a very dangerous and sad situation. 'Still in our twenties we had two children, two suitcases each, and, little more than, two hundred pounds in our pockets. We came at three days' notice as the soccer season was starting.

One month later the caption below captured my mood:

Here I am in the land of plenty My hopes still high but my pockets empty.

Anyone who is tired of America is tired of life.

THE ONLY THING WORSE THAN WORK IS LOOKING FOR WORK.

**You'll know the Irish people, the way they sing and dance and joke
They learn it in their childhood from the little fairy folk.**

Written by the famous Mike Mc Crory, former radio host, 'whistle blower,' Irish football and soccer star, and unforgettable story-teller. Mike and his wife Marie have six children and live in Newport Beach, California.

Contact Author: Michael P. Mc Crory
Tel: 714-916-2362
Email: michaelpmccrory@yahoo.com

iUniverse Publishing.

**Our children are a living message we send
To a time we shall not see.**

In our younger days !

A woman's beauty surpasses all else that charms the eye.

Printed in the United States
by Baker & Taylor Publisher Services